Weekly Strategies for Writers: Tips on Writing, Editing, Publishing, Marketing & more

Linda A. Lavid

Full Court Press
Buffalo, New York

Published by Full Court Press
A division of FCPress
PO Box 342
Buffalo, NY 14223

ISBN-10: 0-9817070-6-8
ISBN-13: 978-0-9817070-6-8
Library of Congress Control Number: 2012934184

Cover photo: Marco Michelini

Printed in the United States of America

Preface

Years ago, I was in a pediatrician's office talking with another woman. We were commiserating about feverish children when I asked how many kids she had. "Five," she said. Awestruck, I blurted, "Five? I can barely manage two." She laughed and said, "It wasn't planned. First, I had one then another. Before long I was in the big numbers." And such became my story…not with children but with books.

So how did I come to publish eight books? It certainly wasn't planned or even imagined. It all began by writing one story. That's it. One story that, three years later, was published in an anthology. And a seed was sown. Not a publishing seed, that came later, much later, but an inkling that if I kept writing I could write and publish yet a second story. Which I did the following year. Then my goal changed: I wanted one page of publishing credits, a platform to approach agents and commercial publishers. I then wrote more stories, which I submitted to magazines, online e-zines and newspapers. Slowly the page filled, but this turned out to be a secondary gain. A symbiotic relationship between my writing and publishing developed: having my work accepted by editors, then seeing it published, gave me the confidence to keep writing, which in turn made me a better writer, which led to more publishing. At last, a Catch 22 with a silver lining – I wrote, I published, to write and publish again.

But this isn't the whole story. I'm a writer living in a certain time where technological confluences have made this journey possible. Some background…

Not so long ago, publishing your manuscript was restricted to finding a publisher or spending thousands of dollars to publish yourself. Thanks to technology, this is no longer the case. Four technological advances have converged allowing many voices of many places the option to write, publish and market their work easily and inexpensively. Specifically, after the original break-through of the personal computer, there came the word processing program, the Internet, Print on Demand technology, and e-publishing. Each innovation closed the gap between author and reader by arming writers with tools to create, edit, publish (print/electronically), and market books. Suddenly, many writers like myself are "all in", taking charge and making money.

Anyway, we each have reasons for publishing our work. They can be grand or parochial. Perhaps you want to test the waters or get your work reviewed or reel in a commercial publisher or make a gazillion dollars. What-ever the reason, publishing your work is a choice filled with opportunity and surprise. To help, I'm passing along *Weekly Strategies for Writers*.

Happy writing *and* publishing! Linda

Introduction

For years I've been immersed in writing and publishing. Along the way, I also began to give talks and teach seminars. My first book on writing fiction and publishing was *Composition: A Fiction Writer's Guide for the 21st Century*. In *Composition*, I presented, in progressive order, the salient points of how to write and publish a great story. *Composition* provides a blueprint for those who wish to write and publish fiction using a subsidy publisher, as opposed to a printing service (Lightning Source/CreateSpace), and is a helpful primer for those who are stalled, overwhelmed, or lost in the process.

This book (and e-book), *Weekly Strategies for Writers*, is a year's worth of weekly tips in bulleted format on the following topics: Writing, Editing, Publishing, Using a Website, and Marketing. *Weekly Strategies for Writers* fleshes out many of the topics discussed in *Composition* but is a stand-alone book formulated from my own questions as I wrote and published. Although the writing sections in this book are primarily geared toward fiction, many of the tips address publishing as a whole. Hyperlinks are included in the e-book that relate to that particular tip. For underlined links from this print book, e-mail me and I'll send along a listing of the links included in this book. (lindalavid@gmail.com)

I considered various layouts for this book and decided to present one weekly tip on each topic, thereby reflecting the dilettante role of every publishing writer where everyday we do a little of this and a little of that.

Writing and publishing is a dynamic process where craft builds and technology morphs. No matter where you are on this continuum, I hope *Weekly Strategies for Writers* will provide valuable and useful information to you, the inveterate, dreaming CEO of one: the independent writer.

Contents

Pacing; Convoluted Tenses; Digital Rights Management (DRM); Animations; Social Bookmarking.

Week Fourteen - 37
Describe with Senses; Boring Verbs; E-Book Conversion; Submit to Directories; Press Release.

Week Fifteen - 39
Sequel; Vary Sentence Structure; Book Distribution; Site Naming; Use Directories.

Week Sixteen - 41
Story Goal; Put Work Aside; BlueLeaf Book Scanning; Having a Dedicated Website; Selling Venues.

Week Seventeen - 43
Get Unstuck; Sparse to Dense Description; Audio Books; External Page Links; Post-Publication Reviews.

Week Eighteen - 45
Read, Read; Concerns and Fixes; Where Does the Book Fit?; Host Freebies; QR Codes.

Week Nineteen - 47
Cause and Effect; Vague Words; Pre-Publication Reviews; Selling Books Offline; Coupons.

Week Twenty - 49
Fact Checking; Avoid Clichés; Book Title; Traffic Ranking; Press Kit.

Week Twenty-One - 51
Leave a Question; Words to Check; How to Start a Publishing Company; Website E-mails; Flyer.

Week Twenty-Two - 53
Characters Per Scene; Weak Modifiers; Rights; Pages Too Wide; Videos.

Week Twenty-Three - 55
Have Feelings Change; Interior Monologue Clean-up; Cost of Updating Digital Book Files; Tone of Website; Goodreads Giveaway.

Week Twenty-Four - 57
Transitions; Feedback/Focus Groups; Back Cover Blurb; Author Websites; Q&A.

Week Twenty-Five - 59
List punctuation; OWL; Sales Tax; Adding Hyperlinks; Tags.

Week Fifty-Two - 113

Be Kind to Yourself; Editing Services; Copyright Infringement; Navigation Links; The Pipeline.

Week One

We know what we are, but not what we may be.
– William Shakespeare

Writing Tip: Of all the tips that follow there is one that reigns supreme, the golden tip. It is from this tip that everything else follows. It is simple and irrefutable: Write a terrific book. A terrific book builds readership and is your best promotion.

Editing Tip: When a reader doesn't know who's talking in a scene, he'll get confused and stop reading. Never give a reader this opportunity. If there are only two characters in a scene but the dialogue runs long, add a few action tags, i.e., *Lola grimaced.* "Get off my case." or *Lola slammed the cupboard door.* "Get off my case." Dialogue with more than two characters can be challenging to write. Explaining who's saying what to whom demands acrobatic skills. From my experience, novice writers, more than veteran writers, tend to write scenes with multiple characters. To simplify dialogue in a dinner scene with eight characters, focus on an intimate conversation between two of them. Best not to transcribe verbiage from fictional guests who've had too much Pinot Grigio.

Publishing Tip: Publish articles online. While not always a paying market, the advantages are many: no mailing costs, quick response time, worldwide exposure, and a publishing credit for your résumé /bio. Before submitting, read site content and follow the submission guidelines. Article Submission

Website Tip: Certain immediate elements on a website can cut a visitor's stay to seconds. This often occurs when a visitor has to wait for the page to load or if the site is uninviting. To address these problems: don't have a stand-alone *enter* page; compress image files (Week

Four); keep background plain; use readable text in a contrasting color from the background; avoid pop-ups, distracting banners, music; have a site that appears organized with clear navigation buttons. Web pages aren't read as much as they are scanned. Headlines, bulleted paragraphs, and clickable links will draw a visitor's eyes.

Marketing Tip: Stuck in traffic? No problem. Advertise to the masses with a bumper sticker of your book or website. Cheap, effective, and easy to design. <u>Bumpersticker</u>

Week Two

Success is the ability to go from one failure to another with no loss of enthusiasm.
– Sir Winston Churchill

Writing Tip: One of the best places to read fast-paced, clipped writing is the sports page. Verbs are especially colorful. Read, highlight, and make them yours.

Editing Tip: To search for those pesky typos, consider reading the work backwards, from the last word on the last page to the first word on the first page. This avoids the natural tendency to skim pages you have read hundreds of times. It works and is especially gratifying when a typo is found. Speaking for myself, not an uncommon occurrence.

Publishing Tip: Knowing the cost of print author copies is critical in making your publishing venture a financial success. Author copies are books purchased from the publisher or printing company for resale by the author. Author copies should be based on the printing costs of the book not on a percentage off the cover price. If you are using a subsidy publisher, this cost can vary greatly. When a company is not specific with the cost of author copies, do not give them your business. Keep in mind when placing your book on consignment in a bookstore, their standard fee is 40% of the cover price. Should author copies cost you 20% off the cover price and your local bookstore is asking for 40% commission, you will lose money.

Website Tip: A FavIcon is a logo that appears along side your URL (web address) in the browser window (where a web address is typed in) when your site is bookmarked. A FavIcon is a simple graphic saved in an image file. For my site, I cropped a flower from a photograph and shrunk it down in a photoshop program. User

13

friendly and no-cost online programs, including clip art, are available to format your logo into HTML language that is first uploaded into your root directory, then embedded into your index/home page. If there are viewing problems, go into your browser's toolbar to Internet Options and delete temporary files, history, cookies, then refresh the page. FYI...A browser is a software application that is necessary to access the Internet, web pages and sites. Most common browsers at this time are Internet Explorer, Mozilla Foxfire, Safari, Chrome, and Opera. Browsers and computers can have different settings and capabilities that then affect how a web page is accessed and viewed. Clip Art FavIcon

Marketing Tip: Keeping track of your news, reviews, and books can be daunting. One way to stay current is to list yourself on Google Alerts. When Google comes across some new information about you, an alert will be sent to your e-mail address. Yes, it is all about you. Also consider doing topical alerts using keywords in areas of interest or expertise. Alerts will provide leads to blogs or postings of potential marketing opportunities. As an example, if your interest is in kayaking, and you come across a kayaking blog, you can approach the blog host about doing an article.

Week Three
People ask for criticism, but they only want praise.
– W. Somerset Maugham

Writing Tip: Add sophistication to your writing with foreign words. So darn easy these days with a translator. Translating programs abound online and are easy to use. Where was this marvel when I was translating the ablative case? Anyway, a sprinkling is fun but overuse can be pretentious or worse, confusing. The adage "less is more" applies. Commonly-used foreign words are not italicized. For instance, niche (commonly used) would not be italicized, but *mais naturellement* would. Common usage can be subjective. When in doubt, italicize.
Translator

Editing Tip: Most word processing programs have a nifty tool that can analyze your writing for: grade level, amount of passive voice (3% or less is recommended for fiction), sentence and paragraph complexity. Since word processing programs store this in different areas, search for analysis or readability.

Publishing Tip: Prepare a bio for book covers and promotions. Highlight experience that relates to your book as well as other published work, awards. Every person who has written a book has a story to tell and a reason why it was written. This can be part of your bio.

Website Tip: Linking to other pages on your site or to external sites is one of the wonders of a website. These links are called hyperlinks. They are underlined and often bolded or in a different color. When linking (Week Twenty-Five), avoid using generic words like *link here* or *click here*. Instead be specific and name the link with descriptive content, i.e., *Eli's photos* or *Copyright Office*. Click on links every few months. If they are dead, delete them. Sometimes you'll find a link that's parked. This means the URL (website name) is being used but may be reorganizing. Link Checker

Marketing Tip: Every author on Amazon is invited to create an author page. Here you can write a bio, add books, see reviews, stream your blog or twitter accounts, and post videos. Sales info is also available. Amazon customers can link to this page by clicking on your name from your book page. Author Central

Week Four
Vigorous writing is concise.
– William Strunk Jr.

Writing Tip: Ernest Hemingway said, "Leave water in the well," meaning at the end of a writing day, stop short so you'll know where to start the following day. This works. Some law of inertia I suspect.

Editing Tip: Line by line editing is the evaluation of each sentence. This type of editing occurs after the story is written, when the plot is set, and the story/article has a beginning, middle and end. Line by line editing is about language and the words used. What to look for...Does the sentence follow logically from the previous sentence? Does the sentence make sense? Are there redundancies (words, meanings, spellings)? Is grammar usage correct? Are there missing words, misspellings, dull language? Line by line editing is careful consideration and takes time. But there's a huge payoff: focusing on small sections of words improves writing ten-fold.

Publishing Tip: When putting together a cover, include the book's genre (Week Twenty-Seven) or subject area. Usually found in one of the four corners of the back cover, this notation is primarily used for filing purposes in bookstores and libraries. However every book is well served by having this moniker for two reasons: subject/genre specification is standard practice with commercial publishing; categorizing your book will draw readers who are interested in that particular topic or genre. Subject areas are delineated from general to specific. Fiction/Mystery; Psychology/Behavior Modification.

Website Tip: A third of visitors exit websites if they have to wait more than 12 seconds. High-speed cable pages load quickly, while dial-up users may have significant wait times. When a page takes awhile to load, image files may be too large. The following links address both concerns. When testing a website with the page speed tool, loading time with different access speeds, such as dial-up, will be shown. The report generated suggests how a site can be streamlined. Slow-loading images can be compressed by going to GiFbot. Compressing an image doesn't make it smaller, only the way the file is saved, i.e., fewer bytes. While fewer bytes can affect resolution, this shouldn't be a problem for thumbnail (small) images. Conversely, a large image file placed on a site will retain its byte size even though it may be made smaller in size. For example, a 400KB picture placed on a site will remain a 400KB picture even if the borders of the image are manipulated to thumbnail size. <u>Page Speed Report</u> <u>GIFbot</u>

Marketing Tip: Blog tours or Virtual Book tours are essentially time-specific postings on other blogs about your book. These postings can be a short interview, a review of your book, a guest post, podcast, video, book trailer (Week Forty-One), excerpt, live chat, article, contest. To entice attendance, offer freebies, like an autographed book. Part of the agreement is for you to advertise your appearance and direct your readers to the blog that is on your tour. Think of it as a five/ten city stop only on the Net. Check out the sites first to see if they may be a good fit, then contact the host. Also consider doing the same for other authors (cross promotion) on your blog.

Week Five

If you don't have time to read, you don't have the time or the tools to write.
– Stephen King

Writing Tip: What makes character? In fiction, as in life, who we are has to do with challenges faced: a new mother, a soldier back from war are qualitatively changed. Inherent in challenge is conflict, the life force of any story. To build conflict make your created world a hazardous place for your protagonist. See him/her cringe, fight, run, lie, lose, and don't let up. Consider levels of conflict: the police want answers, the bank's foreclosing, and dear granny can't be found. Which re-minds me... *At sixty, my grandmother began walking five miles. She's ninety now. We don't know where the hell she is.* – Ellen DeGeneres.

Editing Tip: While tools in word processing programs are not foolproof, they provide another set of eyes. Be-sides grammar and spell checks, a review can catch punctuation errors. Again not all of them, but enough to make a scan worthwhile. When the program highlights a section for review, consider the options offered and the explanations provided. These mini-tutorials can be edu-cational.

Publishing Tip: Free publishing is e-publishing, that is to say electronic publishing. But that's only a small part. There are tremendous advantages: publish quickly; can publish any manuscript length; edit/change at no cost; access global market; receive 70% royalties; have sear-chable text; presentation is user-defined; ability to add graphics, videos, book descriptions, links; allow text-to-speech option; is a green paperless technology with no transportation, warehousing or mailing costs. For more info, see Smashwords (Week Forty-Three), Kindle Digital Platform (Week Thirty-Three).

Website Tip: SEO is the acronym for Search Engine Optimization Finding your site among billions of web pages is improved by optimizing your visibility. There are onsite methods and offsite methods to draw visitors. Onsite methods include identifying each page on your website with a unique title, description and content-rich keywords that are lifted from that page. This info is embedded into the HTML page for search engines to scan. Offsite methods include placing your website URL in online directories or in any articles, blogs, press releases, forums or any other sites where you are identified. These links that point back to you are called back links. The more back links the higher your web pages will be ranked among search engines. <u>Back Link Checker</u>

Marketing Tip: Include links to your website, blog, bookstore in all e-mail signatures. Some e-mail programs allow images, such as a book cover, logo, or YouTube video, which is a great way to catch someone's attention. Also consider a teaser line, like a question or something short and punchy that will encourage a click: *Author throws herself in front of a bus*.

Week Six

It does not matter how slowly you go
so long as you do not stop.
– Confucius

Writing Tip: The manner of storytelling changes with the times. Generally, dense blocks of narration, description, backstory have given way to scene development with interwoven elements of dialogue, description, interior thought, exposition, and narrative summary. Today's popular writing style is characterized by white space on the page indicative of short paragraphs.

Editing Tip: Continuity problems plague fiction and the most astute writer will confuse his lies, i.e, what were blue eyes on page twenty are brown eyes on page eighty. To avoid these problems, visualize a person *en toto* and link characters to actors or someone you know. For instance, in your mind's eye have a character, Uncle Barney, look like Cary Grant. Keeping the two connected should avoid the continuity problem of Barney having a washboard stomach in Chapter Two and a beer belly in Chapter Thirty.

Publishing Tip: An International Standard Book Number (ISBN) is a unique number assigned to your book for efficient, universal cataloging by wholesalers, booksellers, libraries, universities, and distributors. This 13 (or 10) digit number found on a book's back cover is assigned and purchased from Bowker. Blocks of ISBNs are only assigned to publishers, whether they are individuals or companies. These numbers are not transferrable and can not be sold. In most cases, subsidy publishers provide an ISBN, under their company name, as part of their publishing package. ISBN

Website Tip: Whenever an image is placed on your website or blog, give it a good keyword name. Search engines can't see images but do read titles. The title should relate to your site's content to improve visibility on the Net. For instance, if you're placing a picture of your dog, Pinkie, on your dog-grooming site, title the picture, *Perfectly Coiffed Dog*, rather than Pinkie which is too general and non-specific to what you're about.

Marketing Tip: Amazon Associates is an advertising program where product links from Amazon can be placed on your website/blog. When a visitor on your site clicks the link and purchases that product or any other from Amazon within a certain amount of time, you'll receive a small commission. To join Amazon Associates you must sign up. Once approved, select the type of ad (widget) you'd like to run and follow the design directions. When you are happy with the ad, you'll be given a code to place into the HTML of your web page. After the ad is placed onto your site/blog, statistics are available to monitor traffic and sales. Amazon Associates

Week Seven

We turn not older with years, but newer every day.
- Emily Dickinson

Writing Tip: To keep dialogue fresh, use sentence fragments, contractions, and if germane to the character, commonly-used slang: gonna, wanna, y'know. Avoid dialect unless your ear is flawless and you are prepared to be consistent throughout.

Editing Tip: Reduce as/ing constructions. Two examples: 1. *As she walked to the door, she stepped on a nail.* 2. *Walking to the door, she stepped on a nail.* Both sentences describe simultaneous action. When over-used, as/ing statements can fatigue the reader. An easy fix: *She walked to the door and stepped on a nail.* Such constructions can also imply improbable actions. Example: *Walking to the door, she turned the knob.* But if she's walking to the door how can she turn the knob? As/ing phrases are often overused by novice writers. Weeding out these troublesome spots makes writing stronger.

Publishing Tip: Royalty payments are made by a publishing company to an author when his/her book is sold. Royalty percentages vary depending on how a book is published. A commercial publisher usually pays lower royalties since the company absorbs much of the initial publishing costs: editing, cover design, book layout, printing, distribution, marketing, advance. Royalties with a subsidy publisher are contract specific and can differ significantly. The better royalty is either 80% or more of the net profit or 20% or more of the cover price. Subsidy contracts that offer less than fifty percent off the net should be avoided.

Website Tip: HTML is the acronym for Hyper Text Mark-up Language. HTML is one of the languages that formats a website so that it can be read properly by browsers. Basic knowledge of HTML can take you some distance in understanding what all those symbols, darts, and letters mean. In simple terms, HTML consists of nested codes that delineate title, body, line breaks, paragraphs, meta tags, fonts, colors, etc. All coding begins with darts < > and ends with darts and a backslash </ >. Between these darts are commands. For instance to bold a section of text, the HTML code would be <b> Happy Birthday </b>. This would show up as **Happy Birthday** on a web page. Easy-to-understand tutorials are available online. HTML

Marketing Tip: Have sustained, layered advertising by feeding your blog and/or twitter accounts to other sites like Facebook, Goodreads, LinkedIn, Amazon Author Page. Remarkably easy and effortless with Twitterfeed.

Week Eight

Inspiration does exist, but it must find you working.
- Pablo Picasso

Writing Tip: In writing fiction, always know what your characters are feeling, then illustrate that feeling through one or all of the following: dialogue, interior thought, action, description. For instance, if a character is angry, have him shout (dialogue), swear in his head (interior thought), slam a window (action), and/or have something occur in the setting that reflects his mood: shattering glass (description).

Editing Tip: Join a writer's group and have your work read and critiqued. Try not to defend. Simply listen then weigh the comments. In evaluating the efficacy of feed-back consider if the comment stands alone or is re-peated by many people. If recurrent points are made, take them under advisement.

Publishing Tip: Everything written is copyrighted the moment it is set on paper and therefore protected under copyright law. However, to formally copyright material the work must be submitted to the Copyright Office. Should someone plagiarize your work, having a formal copyright would make it easier to litigate. A Poor Man's copyright (mailing it to yourself) is not considered copy-righted by the Copyright Office. Copyright Office

Website Tip: Besides showcasing your work, a web-site/blog can also run ads, which when clicked, will make money. When we think of online ads, we think immediately of Google, specifically, Google's AdSense program. Like most of Google's products, formatting an ad is easy. Ads can be vertical, horizontal, or blocks of different sizes, and made to blend in with your site's colors. Once an ad is created, a code is devised that you then embed into your website/blog. Once embedded,

Google will read your site and devise a list of ads that reflects the content of your site. Feedback on click activity, including income, can be accessed by logging into your AdSense account. <u>AdSense</u>

Marketing Tip: Programs that gather statistics from your website or blog are often automatically installed or can be installed by using Google Analytics. Statistics gather huge amounts of information. Briefly you will be able to see what pages on your site are the most popular (Week Forty-Nine), where the visitors are coming from, and how long they're staying. This information can be used to hone your advertising campaign. <u>Analytics</u>

Week Nine

Ideas are like rabbits. You get a couple and learn how to handle them, and pretty soon you have a dozen.
- John Steinbeck

Writing Tip: How to name a character? Let the story lead the way. For instance an historical novel would call for an historical name, while a contemporary story, a more modern name. Meanwhile made-up names predominate SciFi and Fantasy. To avoid reader confusion, differentiate names. In other words, don't have an Ed and an Edwin as main protagonists. For an unusual contemporary name, consider looking at last names in the phone book, then use the last name as a first name, i.e., Wilson. Name sites abound online. Behind the Name

Editing Tip: A terrific editing tool is a text-to-speech program. These programs can be downloaded for free and are easy to use. Once downloaded, text from your manuscript is copied and pasted into the program. With a click the text is then spoken aloud. This verbatim read-back is extremely helpful in catching missing words, a feature no other word processing tool can effectively perform. PDF documents also have this option. Once a PDF file is open, click View on the toolbar, then Read Aloud in the drop-down menu. Kindle users can also e-mail doc files to their e-reader and have it read aloud. Natural Readers

Publishing Tip: Contracts with subsidy publishers* vary greatly. The ideal subsidy contract will allow you to: maintain all rights (nonexclusive); set the cover price; have a royalty rate of 80% or better on net sales; have input into the size of the book and number of pages; cancel at any time with no stipulations; have your book distributed and available to selling outlets; purchase author copies that are priced from printing costs; not incur any yearly maintenance fees; accept returns. *Subsidy publishers, aka vanity publishers, charge for services and are the middlemen between an author and printing company. My book *Composition* discusses this relationship at length.

Website Tip: It is important to update your website/blog regularly since a site that remains static will fall under the radar screen of search engines. How often is regularly? At least weekly. A website overhaul is not necessary, just a few changes and/or updates will do the trick.

Marketing Tip: "Ping" your website or blog after it's updated. Pinging is similar to raising the red flag on a mailbox and sends out a cyber-message that your site's been updated. Ping

Week Ten

Illusion is the first of all pleasures.
- Oscar Wilde

Writing Tip: A scene is the basic building block of storytelling where two forces collide. If a scene doesn't have action and conflict, it needs to be omitted or rewritten. To evaluate a scene consider the following: who are the characters? what does each character want? how is the conflict between them played out? what's the outcome?

Editing Tip: Two common symbols often used in dialogue are the ellipsis and em-dash. Ellipses are used to signify a trailing off. *"Mary. This is none of..." Laura's eyes filled with tears.* Em-dashes are used when there is an interruption. *"Mary. This is none of— " The door bell rang.*

Publishing Tip: Amazon Update Form is available to publishers and authors who wish to add information about their books. Should you receive a new review or want to place an excerpt of the book, this form can be used. Links to update cover pictures, make corrections of erroneous information, or create a Look Inside book are also found here. <u>Amazon Update Form</u>

Website Tip: What do you put on a website? Certainly content that includes book excerpts, reviews, links to purchase, bio and contact information. But make it interesting. In other words, use your skills as a writer to engage visitors. Think outside the box. For instance, if your fiction takes place in a city, what info can you present that feeds into this topic. If your book is nonfiction, what more can you add that would complement what's already written. As an example, a memoir could include photographs not in the book. Present content clearly (Week One), and set a tone, perhaps friendly or conversational or humorous.

Marketing Tip: Amazon customers can produce how-to guides. This program is called, So You'd Like To (SYLT). Here authors, publishers, or anyone so inclined are encouraged to write an article recommending how a product can be helpful. Think of your book and how someone may find it worthwhile. As an example, the guide for *Weekly Strategies for Writers* could be: So You'd Like to Publish a Book...I'd then support my claim and add links to this book. Amazon SYLT

Week Eleven
It is easy to be brave from a safe distance.
– Aesop

Writing Tip: There is no need to reinvent the wheel when it comes to setting the stage for your story. Use familiar places you know well. Close your eyes and place yourself there. Take the time and absorb details with all your senses. An intimate knowledge of place will make your story ring true.

Editing Tip: Italicize: foreign words not commonly used; snippets of interior thought; to emphasize a word; in titles of complete works such as magazines/journals, books, newspapers, films, television programs, long poems, plays of three or more acts.

Publishing Tip: Maintain records of inventory and all expenditures and income related to publishing your book. An author can use Schedule C and Form 2106 to document profit/loss/expenses on his/her personal in-come tax form. Maintaining comprehensive records substantiates you are running a business rather than a hobby. A self-publishing author can also incorporate (Inc, LLC) for added tax benefits. IRS

Website Tip: Having a blog is another way to increase visibility on the web. Free blogs are easy to set-up and maintain. As an added bonus they are also interactive. Blogs should be about a focused topic that is updated regularly to snag search engines and keep visitors checking in. Ads for monetization and back links to your website or online selling venues can also be added. Zemanta is a terrific tool to make blogs dynamic. Blogs: WordPress Tumblr Blogger

Marketing Tip: Google AdWords is the premier adver-tising model available worldwide to promote whatever you're selling. It is easy to set up and you define the monthly expense. AdWords come in various formats and colors, including banners. You can elect to place your ads on certain sites or identify keywords that Google will then link to sites. Charges are incurred by clicks to your site or ad impressions on sites where your ad is placed. Advertisers are encouraged to run multiple ads to see what draws the most interest and sales, aka conversions. Google ads are used when you advertise your product. Google AdSense (Week Eight) is when you allow Google ads to run on your blog or site. <u>Google AdWords</u>

Week Twelve

A book must be the ax for the frozen sea within us.
– Franz Kafka

Writing Tip: To keep greased and rolling, have a daily word-count or time quota. Writing daily keeps the story fresh and continuous. Start out small if you like – one hundred words or 30 minutes. It's crucial to choose a quota that's doable and measurable.

Editing Tip: Writing numbers is a complicated affair. Here are some basics: 1 to 100 can be written as numerals; numbers twenty-one through ninety-nine are hyphenated; do not mix numerals with numbers: *he had 5 bananas and two apples*; spell out any number if it begins a sentence: *Forty-five years earlier*; plurals of numerals do not have apostrophes: 1960s; write and hyphenate simple fractions (those under 1): two-thirds, one-half; decimals are written in figures: .45; write out the number if followed by o'clock: *five o'clock*; time can also be written in figures: *At 5:15 A.M. the alarm went off*. Writing Numbers

Publishing Tip: A Library of Congress number catalogs your book for libraries. Getting a number is free as long as you have a publishing company. Application is done online, and once the number is received, the number is placed on the copyright page of your book. Upon publication, a print copy must be sent to the Library of Congress. Library of Congress Please note: Having a Library of Congress Control number (LLCN) has nothing to do with copyright.

Website Tip: Increase web presence by joining social networks. Social networks are free and provide a platform to make announcements, join discussion groups, and interact with a wide audience. You can also start your own social network. If your book is on a specific topic, such as cooking or fishing, having a social network with a similar focus can draw people in. Social networks can be topic- or region-specific. <u>Facebook</u>, <u>LinkedIn</u>, <u>Goodreads</u>, <u>She Writes</u>

Marketing Tip: HARO is an acronym for Helping A Reporter Out. HARO is a clearinghouse website used by journalists who are looking for expert advice/input (from sources) for articles they are writing. After a reporter puts in a request for information, it is bundled with other reporter requests and sent to sources in semi-daily e-mails. Both reporters or sources can request to be on this mailing list with a quick and easy sign-up. <u>HARO</u> A great way to let the world know about your expertise and book.

Week Thirteen
Never confuse movement with action.
– Ernest Hemingway

Writing Tip: A good book is paced well. Pacing occurs throughout the story in varying forms and levels. Alternating the main plot with a subplot can give an ebb and flow to the narrative. But there are other pacing tricks. Scene speeds pace, sequel slows it down. Stretches of exposition, description, and interior thought decelerate the scene, but dialogue and dramatic summary rev it to breakneck speed. Short staccato sentences are fast. Long sentences are slow. Also, to prevent the rhythm from becoming stilted, rearrange the placement of the subject, verb and object, and sandwich short sentences between longer ones.

Editing Tip: Avoid verbs that are cluttered with permutations of the verb "to be" that occur in the progressive and perfect forms. In the progressive form "to be" is added to an "ing" verb. Clean up the tense by dropping the "to be" form. Change *he is playing* to *he plays*; *he was playing* to *he played*; he *will be playing* to *he will play*. The perfect form is inundated with has, had, has been, had been, will have, will have been. Ideally stick with active tenses and get rid of "to be" verbs wherever possible. Instead of *He had been seeing her* consider writing *They dated two years earlier.*

Publishing Tip: Digital Rights Management restricts how an e-book can be used. When a digital file is DRM protected, it can not be copied, printed or shared. Before you decide to DRM your e-publications, consider: DRM files can be easily hacked; Readers prefer DRM-free since they have the option to read an e-book across platforms (computer/reader/phone); Passing around an e-book is free publicity; Whether DRM-protected or -free, copyright law and protection remains in effect.

Website Tip: Free animations, those moving bits of clipart, are widely available and easily inserted into a web page. They usually are saved as a .gif ext. (Common image extensions are: .tiff, .jpeg, .bmp, .gif.) Animations are first downloaded and saved to your computer, then uploaded into your website's root directory. Insertion onto the web page is then just a click away. Keep in mind, too many moving, flashing, rolling, jumping doodads can be distracting. Also be careful with the file size. This can adversely affect the time it takes for the page to load. The file size can be found by right clicking on the image, then looking into properties. The lower the KB (kilobyte), the better. Files with MB (megabyte) or GB (gigabyte) are too large. <u>Animations</u> <u>Best Animations</u> <u>GIFbot</u> (site to reduce file size)

Marketing Tip: Social Bookmarking is a way for people to share articles, news, videos, images or whatever they find interesting on the Net. Digg, Reddit, StumbleUpon, Fark, Slash Dot, Del.icio.us are just a few such sites. Whenever you put out a press release or update a blog, you can then submit the link to these sites. Once bookmarked, your page can be viewed by others who may in turn rate it. Good ratings increases visibility and traffic to whatever page is bookmarked. To see the kind of content that catches on, look over bookmarked articles/blogs/press releases that are popular. <u>Social Bookmarking Sites</u>

Week Fourteen

Everyone wants to be Cary Grant.
Even I want to be Cary Grant.
– Cary Grant

Writing Tip: Have characters use their five senses. These senses include what a character sees, hears, touches, tastes and smells. We all, or many of us, or perhaps only me, tend to describe what a character sees. To expand sensory details and freshen the narrative go beyond the visual. Consider a character walking on a windy beach. Do the waves crash onto the shore? (hear) Do grains of sands sting her cheek? (touch) Is the air salty? (taste) Is there a whiff of oiled bodies baking in the sun? (smell)

Editing Tip: Weed out boring and redundant verbs: walk, look, turn. A simple fix is to use synonyms: step, scan, pivot, or better yet describe the action: *His feet dragged along the kitchen floor.* (walk); *Unable to focus, he reached for his glasses. There she stood more beautiful than ever.* (look); *Wanting to leave, he reached for the door. "Please don' t go," she said. It stopped him cold. He faced her.* (pivot)

Publishing Tip: At the present time, there is no universal language for e-readers. Depending on the e-reader, a word processing document must be converted into a different language, such as .epub or .mobi, to be displayed properly. To convert a word processing document (.doc, .wpd .pdf), one can use: <u>Calibre</u>, a free download and/or Mark Coker's <u>Style Guide</u>, a free e-book. This Style Guide also provides information on having a book conversion done for around $30.00 USD, a steal.

Website Tip: List your site in directories. Directories are searchable site listings that categorize websites under certain topics, i.e., Arts, News, Science. To conceptualize, think of directories as similar to telephone books. Sites listed in Internet directories will rank higher when search engines trawl. Last time I checked there were sixty-eight thousand directories. There are Internet services that submit your site to multiple directories for a fee. Another option is to submit your site manually. Popular directories: <u>Yahoo</u>, <u>Google</u>, <u>Open Directory Project</u>

Marketing Tip: A press release is an article of around 400 words that announces any news about you or your book. Start out with a catchy headline that then leads to the body of the article. Often a city and state are identified for local media feeds. A date is not necessary. At the end, identifying information is given, including how you can be contacted. A press release is news and not the place to be overly dramatic. Let quotes do that for you. A press release is used for many reasons. Besides being sent to media outlets and groups, it can be tucked inside books when they are sent out for review and handed out at book signings, book fairs, or any other promotional event. A press release is a marketing staple. <u>Press release</u>

Week Fifteen
A poem begins in delight and ends in wisdom.
– Robert Frost

Writing Tip: Sequel occurs after a scene. It's when your POV character stands back, processes what has happened and decides on a course of action. By nature, a sequel moves the plot forward, tantalizes the reader, slows the pace and provides a transition. A sequel can be as short as a sentence or as long as a chapter.

Editing Tip: Sentence structure, shake it up. Basic sentence structure is composed of subject and verb in that order. Added are objects, adjectives, adverbs, and prepositional phrases. An example: *Robert stood. He walked to the door.* While grammatically correct, a preponderance of this sentence structure deadens the flow of language. Consider the following: *Robert had to leave, the quicker the better. No regrets this time. With feet scraping against the floor, he crossed the room.*

Publishing Tip: Historically, a publishing author's main stumbling block was getting his work distributed, i.e., from where the book's printed into the hands of a reader. The gauntlet that carries books from where books are produced and stored to wholesalers, retailers, libraries, catalogues is a complicated and expensive affair. However with Print-on-Demand (POD) books, distribution streams are in place for books sold online by stores such as Amazon, Barnes & Noble. Whatever manner you publish, be it on your own or through a subsidy publisher, understand how the book will be distributed and how much it will cost. Trade discount for a POD book, that includes distribution, can run anywhere from 40%-70% of the cover price. This charge covers distribution and retail commissions as well as shipping and handling. An E-book has no distribution fees, only a minimal download charge based on byte size.

Website Tip: What's a good name for a website? A book's title, an author's name, a subject area are all contenders. For search purposes, some say a title is best. For multiple books, an author's name is suggested. On the other hand, if you specialize in a certain kind of book, a subject name may be the ticket. There's also the option of having multiple sites. Just keep in mind the more websites, the more updating. Many hosts (companies that provide websites) offer unlimited domains for the price of one. The only expense is paying for the extra URL name which can run around $10 to $35 per year. In any event before deciding, you must check to see if the name is available. To do this go to any search site and type in *Domain Name Search.* Select a site then simply plug in the names you are interested in. If the name is available it will let you know. If the name is already taken, consider adding a word or two to make it unique: **www.fictionbyJohnSmith.com**. Avoid names that are hyphenated, too long, difficult to remember. Extensions such as: .com, .org, .edu, .us, .net, are part of the name. If www.title.com is taken, **www.title.net** could be used.

Marketing Tip: Directories are sites to submit your website (Week Fourteen), but they can also be used for marketing purposes. Directories are categorized by topic and region. As an example, should you want to find a listing of hotels in Bermuda for your travel book, a directory would be easier and quicker to use than a search engine. Search engines ask for keywords that then snag web pages with any of those keywords. Directories, on the other hand, are organized from subject areas that then close in on specifics. To visualize the difference: a directory fishes for trout with a lure; a search engine fishes with a net for whatever it can get. Take a tour of any directory. This should give you plenty of marketing ideas. Yahoo, Google, Open Directory Project

Week Sixteen

Drama is life with the dull parts cut out.
– Alfred Hitchcock

Writing Tip: Every great story is about character want. To start a story in earnest, ask and answer these three questions in one declarative sentence: Who is my story about? What does this character want? What is stopping him from getting what he wants? Once devised, this declarative sentence is also called the story goal. Think of story goal as the magnetic north. From page one until the end of your story, the story goal will be your homing device.

Editing Tip: In the throes of editing, every writer is bound to become weary. Every page, sentence, word has been looked at, considered, tossed aside, added to endlessly. One way to reclaim your sanity, and more importantly some fresh eyes, is to put the work aside for a couple of days, a week, or however long it takes to recharge.

Publishing Tip: If you want to publish a book that is only in hard-copy book format (no digital file), Blue Leaf Scanning will copy each page and convert into digital content that can be used for republication as an e-book, POD book, or any needed digital format. Cost is nominal.

Website Tip: One of the best values online is having a website. For around $5-$7 per month, round-the-clock advertising is at your fingertips. So what's involved? You must rent a URL (website) name and pay a hosting service. (Yes, there are free hosting services but they often have ads and don't stay in business for long.) Discounts are available should you wish to register your website name and sign up with a host for longer periods. The only other start-up cost could be with website design.

However, before spending hundreds of dollars with a web designer, I'd advise trying it yourself. Hosting companies provide programs, templates, and technological support to get you up and running. Instead of using HTML (Hyper Text Mark-up Language) or PHP (Hypertext Preprocessor) computer language, a point and click application such as WYSIWYG (What-You-See-Is-What-You-Get) can be also used. Tutorials on building a site are widely available. KompoZer HTML PHP

Marketing Tip: When we think of retail outlets for books, we think of bookstores. But the venues to sell books extend well beyond the norm. Books sell successfully in bait shops, hotel lobbies, Scottish festivals, hardware and grocery stores, to name a few. Certainly if you have a niche book (topical), consideration should be made in identifying where your potential reader can be found. A writer can also spin her book to spark a reader's interest. For instance, if a novel takes place in a certain city, market it as such. Local stories, articles, history always attract readership.

Week Seventeen

The cause is hidden; the effect is visible to all.
– Ovid

Writing Tip: Inevitably at some point in your story or article, you will stop cold, unsure what to write next. One way to get unstuck is to ask "wh" questions. In storytelling, you can ask such questions as…What is the main character thinking, seeing, feeling, doing? And why is the character responding in this way? In nonfiction, just as we learned in school, make sure all the "wh" questions are answered…who, what, where, when and why.

Editing Tip: Description runs from sparse to dense and all points in between. Depending on the genre, readers have certain expectations about what and how much is described. A hard-boiled mystery calls for sharp details in no nonsense language. Romance descriptions are rife with sensory details. Historical novels and sci-fi can demand pages as new worlds are portrayed. Still, no matter the genre, make description count by cutting out clichés, redundancies, and/or boring details.

Publishing Tip: Audio books are another way of publishing your work. Interest in audio books is steadily growing since they are easily downloaded into an MP3 player or burned onto a CD. There are two ways to record: with a computer voice or with a human voice. Text-to-Speech programs abound where the text of a book is cut and pasted onto the text-to-speech screen then, with a click on start/record, the text is read and recorded. Easy, flawless, but depending on the program, results can be flat and monotone. Odiogo is the best computer voice I've heard to date. The second way to record is by using a human voice. But whose? Should you want to read your own book there's plenty of software to help: microphone, headset, pop screen to pre-

43

vent "P"s from popping, recording software (Audacity), computer. It's also advised that you stand, keep the same distance from the microphone, read slowly, use gestures and modulate your voice. I recorded a short story of mine and it was very difficult not to make a mistake, let alone keep everything in mind. The other option, and perhaps the best, is to have it done professionally with an actor and engineer. Still you may want to give it a try. Odiogo Audacity

Website Tip: To see if an advertising campaign is drawing visitors to your site, go into your site's statistics and look under links from external page. Any campaign that isn't pulling in visitors should be reviewed. If the link isn't familiar, you can click on it to show where it came from.

Marketing Tip: Post-publication reviews can make the difference between a sale or no sale. Also keep in mind the review process can take awhile, often months after publication. Not to worry. Those kind words can be added at anytime to your blog, website, book page, e- or Print-on-Demand book. Reviews can also be placed on press releases, bookmarks, sell sheets, promotional material. There's no deadline in having a book reviewed. I've seen books reviewed three years after publication. Of course there's a downside to all this review business. Reading is subjective and some reviews may be less than stellar. No writer is immune to a bad review. Be brave. Midwest Book Review

Week Eighteen
I just sit at a typewriter and curse a bit.
– P.G. Wodehouse

Writing Tip: Read, read, read. I believe subconscious formatting takes place when we read. The rhythm, beauty, and art of language is a wonder. How can symbols on paper have such power? When you read, challenge and educate yourself. Take a favorite book, highlight and reread pages that mesmerize. Deconstruct sentences by writing them in longhand, then look behind the curtain and make the magic yours.

Editing Tip: If a reader expresses the following concerns, explore the possible reasons. Concern Number 1. If a reader is confused something may have been left out, glossed over, or too many things were happening at once. Concern Number 2. If a reader says something doesn't make sense, information may be extraneous, incomplete, unclear, or the facts are incorrect. Concern Number 3. If a reader is bored, conflict and emotional content may be flat and/or forward movement is stalled due to an overabundance of irrelevant details and long flashbacks. Concern Number 4. If a reader is unsatisfied, storylines and subplots may be underdeveloped or unresolved.

Publishing Tip: To be a successful publisher, the following questions must be asked: Is there a market? Who are the intended readers? How can they be reached? Why would potential readers buy this book? What's the marketing plan? Before moving forward take some time to answer these questions. If these questions are unimportant, publishing your book could become a huge disappointment.

Website Tip: Take advantage of freebies offered by website hosts. Promotional offers can include: advertising dollars with Yahoo, Google and Microsoft; partner-ships with wholesalers; templates for website design; business accounts and credit.

Marketing Tip: Quick Reader(QR) codes are maze-like black and white squares appearing on products. QR codes are read by phones that have QR readers in them. QR codes contain hyperlinks to product information. As an author, you can design a QR code for your Amazon Author page or website/blog for placement on promo-tional material, i.e. business cards, T-shirts, bumper stickers. Free design tools to generate a QR code are widely available online. It is suggested that when coding a URL, shorten it first (using <u>Bitly</u>), so the code is simp-ler and easier to scan**.**

Week Nineteen

Fiction was invented the day Jonah arrived home and told his wife that he was three days late because he had been swallowed by a whale.
– Gabriel García Márquez

Writing Tip: A concept called cause and effect is the internal integrity of the story that provides a logical framework and forward motion. Cause and effect occurs at every level of a story's construction, from sentence to paragraph to page to chapter. Problems occur when: cause has no effect, effect has no cause, the effect precedes cause, or when there is simultaneous cause and effect. Some examples…Cause with no effect: *He flipped the switch and looked into her cold blue eyes*. What is the effect of flipping the switch? Looking into her cold eyes? To follow cause and effect it should read: *He flipped the switch.* **Light flooded the room.** *He looked into her cold blue eyes.* Effect with no cause: This occurs when a character acts or reacts for no apparent reason, i.e., furious to calm with no transition. Effect precedes cause: *He shot three times after pulling out the gun* should read *After pulling out the gun, he shot three times*. Simultaneous cause and effect: *Ripping off the sheet, she collapsed onto the bed.* This sentence implies that two events are happening at the same time which, when imagined, seems unlikely. Better stated: *She ripped off the sheet and collapsed onto the bed.*

Editing Tip: Weed out vague words such as: thing, something, stuff, aspect, area, factor, unit, situation, type, way, sort of, kind of, nice, a lot of, manner, ideas, activity, procedure, or any general word or phrase that tends to be overly inclusive. To remedy, either omit or replace with specific descriptive words.

Publishing Tip: Pre-publication reviews are usually found on the back cover of the book or in the beginning of an e-book. Often they are extracted blurbs. Getting reviews before publication can put everything on hold. Not just in the time it takes, but once returned, they have to be edited, formatted, and placed wherever you'd like them to appear. If there are time constraints, a fee may be charged. Different reviewers ask for different formats. Some want an (ARC) Advance Review/Reading Copy (Week Twenty-Eight), others are okay with a digital copy. Whatever format you send, make sure it is fairly clean of typos and formatting problems. Another way of handling reviews is to find other authors, specialists in the field, or enthusiastic readers to say a few words. People enjoy seeing their name in print and if they like your book, it's a win-win situation.

Website Tip: Selling books directly to readers from your website is often the most profitable. For this reason, make book sales quick, easy and affordable. Showcase your books on the landing page with clear links to your bookstore or checkout. At checkout, offer payment options that allow for check or credit card. Put books on sale as well as an offer to sign. Once a sale is made, ship quickly with a thank you note and/or promotional freebie, i.e., bookmark, pen. For practices to avoid when selling from your website see Week Twenty-Nine. PayPal Google Checkout

Marketing Tip: Should you publish with Smashwords (Week Forty-Three), take advantage of their coupon program. Smashwords allows any author to format coupons for their e-book(s). Coupons can be for free downloads or for a percentage off the cover price. For instance, if a reader has an iPad and is interested in reviewing your e-book, you can email him a coupon for a free download; or if you'd like to offer a discount of your book from your website/blog, you can place the coupon on the site. Coupons can be time-limited and are easy to design.

Week Twenty

If you don't risk anything, you risk even more.
– Erica Jong

Writing Tip: Whether you are writing fiction or nonfiction, facts must be checked for veracity, correctness and to avoid liability. To accomplish this writers need to be well informed about their topic and/or the have the ability to research. Without question, the Internet is a tremendous help. Resources I commonly use are Google Books, Google/Yahoo images, MapQuest, Ask, Wikipedia as well as keyword searches on search engines. Within five minutes, I've found the lyrics to Elvis Presley's "Blue Suede Shoes" and the date of the last home game of the Chicago Bulls in 2003.

Editing Tip: You've heard it a million times. But it happens to the best of us and nobody's perfect. We're only human. After all everyone has the right to make mistakes. Besides what doesn't destroy us makes us stronger. In summary, avoid clichés like the plague.

Publishing Tip: When selecting the title for your book, consider the following: Can it be remembered? A long title may be forgotten or only partially called to mind, and if a reader doesn't know your name, she may not find your book. What's the genre? Titles of a specific genre may have a similar feel or mood to them. Mysteries appear to have a preponderance of words such as *dead, deadly, night, the mystery of, the case of, the cat who*. Romance titles, on the other hand, have words like *love, kisses, bride*. Is the title unique? No one can own the copyright to a title, so you'll find books with the same title. However, this could pose a problem when someone searches for your book. What makes some titles stand out? Often there's an incongruence to a title, like *Lovely Bones*. Also, think metaphorically. If you've written a mystery about a family secret, what else could express

49

that same idea? A pearl? A locket? The best title may be located within your story in a line of dialogue or a character's name.

Website Tip: Websites are given traffic rankings by search engines. The higher the ranking, the better. Finding your rank, as well as testing and evaluating other aspects of your website, i.e., search position, link popularity, keyword analyzer, Google page rank, is a click away. Webmaster Tools

Marketing Tip: Every book published should have a press kit, a.k.a. marketing kit. A press kit is presented to any venue that sells, advertises, or has the potential to create a buzz about you and your book. A press kit only demands a little bit of your time and energy to create. Each item in a press kit can be used separately and throughout the life of the book. A press kit is displayed in a folder and can include: a business card, press release (Week Fourteen), flyer (Week Twenty-One), Q&A (Week Twenty-Four), promotional material (Week Twenty-Nine) and, if requested, a book. For e-books, all the above could be in digital format.

Week Twenty-One
Not all who wander are lost.
– J. R. R. Tolkien

Writing Tip: To write riveting copy, know where you're leading the reader. Ask the following…What does the reader know? What's the next critical piece he needs to know? Whether fiction or nonfiction, be cognizant of the hook that is being trawled and understand when to let it sway or jerk. Whenever there is a break, i.e., at the end of the chapter or section, leave an unanswered question or impending doom.

Editing Tip: Three editing basics…1. Words to check to see if they're used properly: your, you're; their, there, they're; lie, lay (present and past tense of to lie); lay, laid (present and past tense of to lay); farther (distance), further (time or quantity). 2. Delete unnecessary verb add-ons: *He jumped up* change to *He jumped.* 3. General sharpening: *He started to run* change to *He ran*; *She began writing* change to *She wrote*.

Publishing Tip: Steps to start a publishing company are: check with the locality to see if there are any restrictions; decide on a name; register your business with locality/state; file papers if you incorporate (LLC, Inc.)(Week Thirty-Nine); secure a web address; purchase ISBNs (Week Six); have the software necessary to layout a (e-)book.

Website Tip: Multiple e-mails come with a website and different e-mails can be placed throughout your site. Prominently display the e-mail address or e-mail link on each page for easy accessibility. Website e-mail can be forwarded to your regular e-mail address. This allows a certain level of privacy. However, should you reply to the e-mail from your non-website address, this privacy will be compromised. Besides multiple e-mail accounts, auto-responders, spam detection and mailing list management options are usually offered.

Marketing Tip: Compose a flyer. A flyer, a.k.a. sell sheet, is a page that can be scanned quickly. Instead of a narrative, bullets are used. A picture of the book can be included. Depending who you want to reach, the information on a flyer may change. For instance, a flyer sent to a bookstore is different from one given to a potential reader. A sell sheet to a bookstore should include the discount, how the book is presently being marketed and how it can be ordered. A flyer to a reader would include where the book can be purchased, reviews, cost and a short bio. On the other hand, if you want the opportunity to speak to a group, topics to be discussed would be included. Always indicate how you can be reached. When thinking about a flyer put yourself in the place of that group or person whose attention you want to snag. What would he want to know? What makes you the perfect person to contact? Then say it succinctly in bold, readable print.

Week Twenty-Two
Caress the detail, the divine detail.
– Vladimir Nabokov

Writing Tip: When considering the number of characters in a scene: less is more. Conflict is portrayed and heightened with more clarity and punch when there are two, and only two, opposing characters. When more characters are roaming around, the writer runs the risk of diluting the struggle or confusing the reader, fault lines that once rattled can stop the reader from reading.

Editing Tip: Read sentences and evaluate weak modifiers. In most cases deleting them will not change the meaning of the sentence. A short list of weak modifiers are: almost, actually, very, quite, really, just, truly, seeming to be, even, certainly, so, exactly, anyway, such, definitely, some, few, a little, rather, usually, probably, perhaps, sort of, fairly, somewhat.

Publishing Tip: Rights are ownership of your work. There are different kinds of rights – print, electronic, foreign, movie, audio, worldwide – that can be passed from author to publisher. Nonexclusive rights are rights that remain with the author and are not given to the publisher. Exclusive rights are granted by the author to the publisher. It's important to read the entire contract. Rights can be granted in more than one area of the contract. An advantage for writers who publish without a commercial or subsidy publisher is that they maintain all rights at all times.

Website Tip: When designing pages on a website, avoid having pages that are so wide a visitor as to scroll across. Since visitors have different monitors, it's recommended that no web page be wider than 700 pixels.

Marketing Tip: Videos. I've noticed a proliferation of

YouTube videos on authors' websites. Some have the author talking, others have people reviewing the author's book. Both very effective in a way I wouldn't have expected. Computers now come ready with microphones, cameras, and easy one-click operation. Editing software such as Microsoft Movie Maker or Apple iMovie are also available. Videos don't have to run long, three to five minutes is good. (In most cases, videos longer than ten minutes will not be accepted by YouTube.) Two aspects to consider are delivery and content. How you come across in a video matters. Likeability, sincerity, looking into the camera, speaking in a clear voice with a conversational style, are important. If you can add humor, visuals, even better. Then there's content. So what do you say? Whatever you can be passionate about. It could be about the book or about why you wrote it or humorous anecdotes about having written a book. Once your video is finished, uploaded it to YouTube. Make sure you place tags or keywords for search purposes. From there cut and embed the given code into your website, blog, Amazon Author Page, email signature, and/or add a hyperlinks to the video on YouTube. YouTube

Week Twenty-Three
You drown not by falling into a river,
but by staying submerged in it.
– Paulo Coelho

Writing Tip: A character with emotional ups and downs makes a scene interesting. If a character is bored, by the end of the scene, have her engaged. If a character starts out happy, have circumstances make her sad. This type of manipulation makes change occur, essential in a scene. Also, emotional content hooks a reader and heightens the drama. The only caveat is to express one emotion at a time. In other words, don't make a character actively lonely and angry and revengeful. Decide on one emotion that then changes to another. To up the ante, show her feelings rather than state them.

Editing Tip: Getting into a character's head is the magic in fiction. Except for voiceovers in film and plays, it's the only art form that portrays internal thought. In editing thoughts, evaluate frequent snippets of thought between lines of dialogue or short narration. If they cut into the flow, remove as many as possible. Thought punctuation: never place inside quotes; for brief thoughts, either italicize (*What a loser.*) or use a tag (What a loser, she thought.) Be consistent with punctuation and don't mix italics with tags (*What a loser*, she thought.) For interior monologue that runs longer than a couple of sentences, make it a stand-alone paragraph.

Publishing Tip: No matter how well a manuscript is edited, there are bound to be typos. Naturally, if you had a large number of offset books printed, this is a nightmare. On the other hand, updating or correcting mistakes in a POD book or e-book**Error! Bookmark not defined.** are significantly easier, inexpensive and quicker. Still, costs can vary should you publish through a subsidy or pay someone to edit the book for you. If not specified in their contract, ask how much the subsidy charges to update the digital files of your book. This expense could be twofold: an hourly rate to make the edits and, if a Print-on-Demand book, the cost charged by the printer. At this time, Lightning Source (a POD print company) charges $37.50 each for edits to either the cover or interior files, CreateSpace (a POD print company) charges nothing. E-books can be edited at no cost if you do them yourself.

Website Tip: The tone of your website can attract or repel visitors. Since we're in the bookselling business, friendly, conversational language, humor, relevant and updated content go far in establishing rapport. Sharing information about your books, i.e., where they take place along with pictures, can be entertaining and interesting. To further personalize the site, answer questions and encourage visitors to contact you about your work. Profanity, the hard sell, or impersonal copy (press release), may cut a visitor's stay to seconds.

Marketing Tip: Offering a giveaway on Goodreads is free advertising and a way to get a book reviewed. A book can be entered in the giveaway program six months before or after publication, and there is no limit on how many books a publisher/writer can offer. Once the giveaway ends and readers are selected, print copies are sent by mail. Readers are encouraged to review the book, but my response for reviews has been less than fifty percent. Still, I have found it worthwhile. Goodreads

Week Twenty-Four

A word after a word after a word is power.
– Margaret Atwood

Writing Tip: Seamless transitions can be applied by using… Emotion: *He was angry, so angry he'd blow her head off. By the time the police came he was still angry.* Weather: *The hail pelted against the window. When the sun came out, he headed for the barn.* Dialogue: *He'd have to talk to her. "What do you want?" she said through the crack in the door.* Name: *Clearly, the missing link was Kara in Apartment 3C. She was taller than he imagined. And not so young.* Time: *Two days later the phone still hadn't rung.*

Editing Tip: Once your manuscript is finished, have someone read it. But who? Perhaps someone in your writer's group or someone who reads a lot. Someone who you can reasonably trust and who'll be honest. You can also develop a focus group. A focus group, ideally six to ten participants, is a group interview where everyone meets at the same time and place to discuss your manuscript. To stay on track have an agenda of five or six questions to ask. Focus groups can meet regularly or one time only, usually for about two hours. Each participant will need a copy of your manuscript beforehand.

Publishing Tip: A brief summary of your book is mandatory for back covers, promotions, online book pages, and any number of other uses. Summaries can run a couple of sentences or be presented in short cropped paragraphs. You'll want copy that can be scanned quickly and that has enough punch to make a potential reader take the next step – crack open the book. In fiction, conflict or a character's dilemma should be clear, but the ending should not. A good description intrigues the reader but leaves her wondering. Ask questions or leave a trailing sentence. Effective copy relates an interesting story with a universal theme: *Left for dead on an island, Marcela struggles against mounting odds. Once pampered by a life of privilege, she now scrounges for water, food, shelter. Amid the strife, will her body, heart and soul survive?* Read book summaries of a similar genre. When you come up with a summary, show it around to get response. Once you've settled on the copy, make sure there are no typos.

Website Tip: Check out successful authors' websites and see what they're doing. What catches your interest? Follow their lead.

Marketing Tip: A question and answer (Q&A) sheet is a self-interview. It's commonly sent along with a press release to media outlets, i.e., television, radio, print, on-line. A *Q&A* sheet is useful for two reasons. First, disclosing information about yourself may intrigue a reporter to do a story on you. Secondly, it provides a script should you be interviewed. To get started, consider the following…When did you begin writing? Why did you write this book? Who are your favorite authors? Have you ever had writer's block? How do you write? What is this book about? As you answer these, other questions may come to mind. A self-interview runs around two pages.

Week Twenty-Five
No pen, no ink, no table, no room,
no time, no quiet, no inclination.
– James Joyce

Writing Tip: When devising a list of no specific order use bullets. When there's a hierarchy to the list, use numbers or letters. Single words (not capitalized) on paragraphed lists are separated by commas. Clauses (not capitalized) on paragraphed lists are separated by semi colons. Full sentences (first letter capitalized) on paragraphed lists have periods.

Editing Tip: Online information for MLA or APA formatting, research, citation, grammar, and all your general writing questions, check out the site map at <u>Purdue OWL</u>.

Publishing Tip: If you live in a state that has sales tax, you must make an application for a sales tax ID number. Sales tax is charged and collected for every book sold directly to a customer. When your book is sold on consignment by a store, the store collects the sales tax. In New York State, if you don't make any sales in a quarter/year, you must still file, otherwise there's a penalty: $50. Your business name and ID number can be your name and social security number. If incorporated, you need to have a tax identification number. This is not the case for some Limited Liability Companies (LLC).

Website Tip: Hyperlinks are underlined links that, when clicked, take you to a spot within the site or to a different site. The easiest way of adding a hyperlink is by using the chain icon. This icon is found amidst the tools when a web page is in edit mode. For linking to another site or another page on your site, first go to the page you want to link to and copy the address from the browser. Once copied go back into your website to the page you'd like the link to be placed. It's always good practice to name a link rather than say *Click Here.* If you're linking to a recipe on another site, write *Banana Bread,* then highlight the word, *Banana Bread.* The next step is to click on the chain icon. A drop down menu will appear with a box. In this box, paste the URL you just copied from the browser. Click insert, and the box should close. *Banana Bread* should now be underlined and when clicked send you to the other site. Whenever you update a web page it must be saved for the changes to occur. Instead of a chain icon, some website design programs have *Insert* on a toolbar. Click on *Insert* and a dropdown menu will appear that lists – *Link*. In the dialog box, paste the address that you've copied from the browser. Again always save. Should you then check your website and not see the update, refresh the page.

Marketing Tip: Tags are searchable keywords or short phrases that identify pieces of information that draw traffic to that item. Whenever a video, an article, a review, or information about you or your book is placed online, there is often an option to provide tags. Tags are separated by commas and can be pulled directly from content or be descriptive. Quick and easy, such indexing shouldn't be ignored.

Week Twenty-Six

In order to attain the impossible, one must attempt the absurd.
– Miguel de Cervantes

Writing Tip: The writing concept of an inverted pyramid comes from the smoked-filled rooms of newspaper journalists. Essentially this principle states that the most important point of any article should be at the top, followed by other crucial points in descending order. While a rubric for journalists, fiction writers can likewise take heed. Naturally, riveting copy should start every short story or novel, but there are beginnings beyond the first page. Start new scenes and chapters with the same flair.

Editing Tip: Flashbacks. By nature a flashback stops all forward movement by going into the story's past. Writers often use this devise to illuminate a character's background or motivation. If the flashback is critical to the plot, consider starting the story at that point. When editing, ask the following questions: How many flashbacks are there? How long are they? Can the information be interspersed in the real time of the story? Should the story begin earlier?

Publishing Tip: To design a cover you'll need a Photoshop program. The week that I attempted my first cover, my eyelids were in a perpetual state of twitch. However, once I gained an understanding of the layer function, it was smooth sailing. Think of layers as transparencies that sit on top of each other. Different layers can be turned on or off, added or deleted, as you play with color, graphics, text, and special effects. This gives you tremendous control of the design, without having to start over. There are many sites online that offer copyright free material, such as photographs, clip art, etc. If you have a digital camera, the image bank is infinite. One picture can be cropped, colored, and transformed in unique ways. I recently found software specifically for book cover design. A bit pricey. As time goes on, this kind of software may become less expensive. To get started consider downloading a free trial version of Adobe's Photoshop Elements or the free program, <u>GIMP</u>.

Website Tip: Submit your site to search engines. Web hosts usually offer this free service. Look into your host's home page that automatically loads when you log in. Under services or software or promotional, look for search engine or search engine submission. Click on the icon and simple instructions should follow. These search engine submission programs send your site to many engines. Manual submission is another option. Once your site is indexed by a search engine, increased traffic should follow. FYI...A search engine, like Google, gathers bits of information throughout the web. Automated programs like spiders, robots, crawlers are sent into the wild where they copy the contents of billions of web pages. Once that information is relayed back, the search engine indexes and ranks the content. When a person goes to a search engine and types in keywords, lists of websites with those same words are populated. The websites that come up in response to the keywords are based on the index and rank that the search engine has given those sites. <u>Search Engine Submission</u>

Marketing Tip: Often what separates those who sell and those who don't, lies in response. Not the response of potential buyers, but in the seller's response. If your campaign has never gotten off the ground or is stalled or you don't have any idea why nothing's happening, respond, react and make some changes. Marketing plans often must be tweaked. Try it one way, then another. An aside...Thomas Edison tried six thousand different carbonized fibers for the light bulb.

Week Twenty-Seven

I don't do drugs. I am drugs.
– Salvador Dalí

Writing Tip: In my opinion writer's block, that unexplainable, inability to write is caused by either a lack of craft or being overly critical. Lack of craft is remedied by writing. For being overly critical: lower your standards, loosen up, and keep plugging away.

Editing Tip: Prepositions are abstract words that specify place, direction, and time, i.e., into, beneath, during. They are an integral part of language but an overabundance of prepositional phrases is a clear sign to reevaluate and tighten. *He walked from the kitchen into the living room and sat on the couch,* can be changed to: *He left the kitchen and sat on the couch.* Okay, the edit isn't drop-dead copy, but it cuts to the chase. Consider circling the prepositional phrases on a page of copy. Make them visible then pluck them out.

Publishing Tip: Genre is the kind of story you're telling. Some genres are: romance, mystery, sci-fi, fantasy, horror, literary. And within these genres there are sub-genres. As an example, a romance could be contemporary, historical, erotic or suspense. While crossing genre lines – time-travel horror, mystery sci-fi – has become more acceptable, defining the basic genre is important since genres attract readership. A mixed-genre classification, such as horror-sci-fi, may turn off potential readers who gravitate toward conventional types of stories.

Website Tip: Attracting new visitors to your site is important but so is keeping the visitors you already have. Think of most people's purchasing behaviors. They look something over, leave, do a little comparison shopping, then return and look at it again. Return visitors are important and every effort should be made to keep them coming back. How? By updating content. How often? A couple times a week. Yes, it's a commitment...totaling half an hour.

Marketing Tip: When selling in person be friendly, enthusiastic, and maintain good eye contact. Speak clearly and smile. Ask questions. Present an attractive display where your book can be picked up and scanned. Have reviews readily available and the price of the book in clear sight. Encourage readers to take the book, look it over and bring it back. Offer free gift-wrapping. For any function where there are crowds, raffle off a reader's basket (books, chocolates, coffee cup). On the raffle stub ask for an e-mail address and if it would be okay to contact them with any further promotions. When signing a book, make sure the inscribed name is spelled correctly. A book is signed on the title page with the date noted.

Week Twenty-Eight

I am not afraid of storms for I am learning how to sail my ship.
– Louisa May Alcott

Writing Tip: Introducing a character should be like meeting someone in real life. Perhaps some descriptive detail catches your attention – the way she's dressed, the color of her eyes. What comes next? The tenor of her voice, a quirky mannerism? Over-describing a character when she first comes onto the scene is not true to life. However, there is one exception. When a character is discussed by other characters, suspense can build. Yes, there is a place for gossip in storytelling.

Editing Tip: What's the word count of your manuscript? Generally, the word count of an average novel runs 60K (thousand) to 100K, a novella anywhere between 20K to 60K, a short story 1K to 20K, flash fiction below 1000 words. If you are marketing your manuscript as a novel and need to beef up the word count, consider adding another level of conflict for your protagonist. Conversely, if your manuscript is unruly and well beyond 100K, consider cutting characters and those subplots attached to them.

Publishing Tip: Advance Reader/Review Copies (ARCs) are printed books sent out by large publishing companies to reviewers prior to publication. They are not the final proofed or bound copy. Due to POD technology, writers can now take advantage of having an ARC of their book to look over and, if they wish, send out for reviews before the manuscript is formally published. For a nominal fee, a digital file of your manuscript can be uploaded to Lulu, where it can be formatted into a book, then ordered and used as an ARC. Lulu

Website Tip: Maintain a backup copy of your website in

your computer and flash drive. Host services include downloading and uploading capabilities. Software to download websites is also available online. As web pages are updated and changed, problems can occur when coding inside the pages are toyed with. Should the page you're working on become a morass of weirdness, rest easy, the original page can be uploaded.

Marketing Tip: Provide increased shopping options by placing a shopping cart on your site. PayPal is a widely-used shopping interface for worldwide selling and buying online. PayPal's Website Payments Standard has no monthly, set-up or cancellation fees. The seller sets the price of products as well as the shipping and handling charges. State sales tax can also be applied. PayPal accepts many types of payments and, since it is a third-party company, buyer and seller information remains confidential. PayPal is paid a commission when a product is sold. Opening a Website Payments Standard account is easy. After that, you select a PayPal button and define your product. A code is then provided that you copy and embed into your website. Another shopping cart is available from GoogleCheckout. In many ways similar to PayPal, their commission is less and can be free should you advertise with GoogleAdwords. Google Checkout PayPal

Week Twenty-Nine
The mere attempt to examine my own confusion
would consume volumes.
– James Agee

Writing Tip: Perfection is overrated and boring, therefore give your protagonist a flaw. A character's shortcoming not only makes him interesting but can add tension. Alfred Hitchcock's *Vertigo* is a prime example. The protagonist has a fear of heights, that same fear he must deal with during the climax of the story. Flaws, besides psychological, can be physical, emotional. Again, don't overdo. A neurotic character is good; a basket case, not so much.

Editing Tip: When the word *that* is followed by an independent clause (a clause with a subject and verb), the *that* should be deleted. Change *She trashed the ring that he had given her* to *She trashed the ring he had given her.*

Publishing Tip: Book Sections. Taken from *The Chicago Manual of Style* the sections of a book are divided into front matter and back matter. In order, front matter includes: Title page, Copyright notice, Dedication or Epigraph, Contents, Lists of Illustrations/Tables, Foreword, Preface, Acknowledgements, Introduction. In order, back matter includes: Appendix, Notes, Glossary, Bibliography, Contributors, Index. A foreword is usually written by a specialist in the field. A preface is written by the author and discusses the reasons why the book was written. An introduction is about the book itself. Epilogues, Afterwords and Conclusions are considered part of the interior text and are placed before the back matter.

Website Tip: When selling books directly off your website avoid: high shipping charges; overpriced items; *buy* buttons as opposed to *order* buttons (*buy* buttons make customers feel obligated); unnecessary scrolling; a checkout process that requires too much personal information; tallying the total cost including shipping/handling/tax after the purchaser buys the item.

Marketing Tip: Promotional material can be brochures, business cards, bookmarks, pens, magnets. Giveaways should be colorful and, if possible, useful – something that won't be tossed out. Consider adding text that may be of interest to a reader, i.e., a quote from a famous book or writer. Contact information, such as your website, should be branded onto every item. Promotional material doesn't have to cost a lot of money. I upload designs to fit on templates at a business card site and am able to get lots of stuff for a fraction of the cost, especially during their free promotions. Bookmarks can be designed on a computer then mounted and presented in many unique ways. To avoid the cost of color printing, use colored paper. VistaPrint

Week Thirty

A primitive artist is an amateur whose work sells.
– Grandma Moses

Writing Tip: Conceptualizing a story can grow from a listing of potential climatic moments to pages of chapter summaries. The format can be a narrative, in bullets, flow charts, on cards, or a combination of all of the above. The important thing is to write down some type of outline, rather than leave it swimming amorphously in the head where it can be forgotten or overwritten.

Editing Tip: The apostrophe**Error! Bookmark not defined.**. Who invented this wonder? Not always intuitive, the apostrophe is rife with dos and don'ts. Basically, the apostrophe is used to: form possessives of nouns (boy's hat), show omissions of letters (don't), indicate plurals of lowercase letters (p's and q's). Often these rules are incorrectly generalized and before long apostrophes are flying like confetti. For instance, while plural lowercase letters call for an apostrophe, symbols (%s), numbers (1960s) and capital letters (RSVPs) do not. When doing final edits, search for apostrophes then determine if they're properly used. Running the grammar/spell check tools in your word processing program can also help. Lastly, always know the difference between *its* and *it's*. *It's* is a contraction for it is. *Its* is a possessive form of it (*with its head held high*).

Publishing Tip: Blank pages in a print book are determined by the measurement of pre-cut paper sheets. Due to paper size, how the paper is cut and printing method, the number of pages in a book can be figured in multiples of four, eight, sixteen or thirty-two. If your book runs 129 pages and is printed in multiples of eight, the actual number of pages will be 136. This means you will have seven extra blank pages. To utilize these pages, place reviews or an author biography before the title page or add excerpts and promotional information for other books at the very end. Blank or printed pages cost the same so make the most of them.

Website Tip: Freeware (no-cost software) abounds for every aspect of website design and maintenance. Freeware is often rated by users. Rather than be overwhelmed by the available programs, check out their reviews first. Shareware is software that can be downloaded and tried before purchase. Both freeware and shareware are often on the cutting edge of new technologies. Even standard programs, i.e., Adobe Acrobat 8, can be downloaded for a trial period. Freeware Shareware

Marketing Tip: Amazon's Listmania is a marketing tool where writers can develop a list of books (including their own), that will then be placed on other book pages. An author has no control when or how often the list may show up, but it's worth the small effort to take advantage of this free advertising opportunity. Keep in mind, listing your book with only bestsellers will put your list in a queue that may or may not be posted. One book can be placed on many lists. Listmania lists are stored automatically on your profile page and can be edited or deleted at any time. Some guidelines: List books similar to yours. Could be of a similar genre, time period, place. Make many lists for any one book. Again, think of genre, place, etc. Do a list for every published book. Attract readers with a catchy title. Include credentials to show others your expertise in developing such a list. Explain how your list can be used. Share your list with friends. Do lists with other authors. Listmania

Week Thirty-One

Easy reading is damn hard writing.
– Nathaniel Hawthorne

Writing Tip: What's the timeframe of the story? Does the story transpire in days, years, or a lifetime? When does the story begin? The sooner you get a handle on the timeline of the story, the fewer continuity problems you'll have. If not done from the outset, recreating a timeline can be tedious. While critical to every story, the importance of time varies. A contemporary story may only need general references to time, but the time element in a mystery or a historical novel is crucial to plot. Setting up suspects/alibis or anchoring the narrative in real events, demands a precise timeframe.

Editing Tip: *Had* (past perfect) describes an action that took place before another past action. Too many *hads* on a page refer to events long over and stops all forward movement of a story. Some fixes...Write the past perfect as a contraction, he'd, she'd. Start the paragraph with a had, then switch to simple past: *But he had loved her. Back in high school when his expectations were simpler – their walks by the river, late night kisses on her parent's porch. But that was then.* Change the past perfect to the simple past: *Did he ever love her? Sure, maybe back in high school...*

Publishing Tip: Some basics on print book layout...Headers are usually capitalized but may be up to two points smaller than the text font size. Pages on the left side (verso) are even-numbered, pages on the right side (recto) are odd-numbered. Title (nonfiction) or author name (fiction) is placed on the left header. Chapters (nonfiction) or book titles (fiction) are on the right header. New chapters often begin on the right page. Chapter titles start a third- or half-way down the page. A minimum of half-inch margins should be formatted on all sides. Standard paperbacks are, in inches, 5x8, 5.5x8.5, 6x9. Perfect bound books are used for most sizes. Saddle-stitched bindings can be used for books up to 50 pp. E-books do not have page numbers or headers.

Website Tip: Whenever you are stuck, frustrated or have questions about any aspect of website design, use or maintenance, go to any search engine and ask a question or type in keywords that describe your concern. Answers and help are a click away.

Marketing Tip: Podcasts are digital media files (audio/video) that are sent over the Internet. They can also be downloaded into your computer or MP3 player. Media sites transmit podcasts for live listening (streaming) or for downloading to review at a subscriber's convenience. Radio stations and other media outlets, broadcast interviews, news clips, on digital media but individuals can as well. With a computer and microphone, you can talk about your book or be interviewed by a friend, record it on your computer, then upload the file to your website/blog or place it on a site that broadcasts podcasts. A recent program that's hit the airwaves is Odiogo. Odiogo can be placed on your blog for read back as well as downloaded to be listened to at your convenience. Essentially, it's a text-to-speech program using a computer voice. Audacity Podcast Odiogo

Week Thirty-Two
Discontent is the first necessity of progress.
– Thomas A. Edison

Writing Tip: A tighter more riveting story will usually be told from one perspective or POV. This reflects the human condition since we experience life from one perspective. The most common styles of POV are expressed in first person or third person subjective. Both these styles are limited to being inside a character's head, either in the *I* form or the *He/She* form. The *I* form is a bit more constricting but intimate. The *He/She* form allows for more narrative but there's a distancing as well. There is also an omniscient POV where there are multiple perspectives. Difficult to pull off without confusing the reader, this POV is reserved for veteran writers.

Editing Tip: The modality auxiliary verbs of *can* and *could* have present tense usages. Can is used to described an ability: *I can swim*; or a willingness: *Can you pass the butter?;* or a possibility: *There can be many explanations*. *Could* is used in the present tense when it denotes a conditional tone: *Mary's not here, she could be at the store.*

Publishing Tip: Due to technology, full-color books and e-books can be published at a reasonable cost with professional results. Full-color books are a great way to showcase artwork or produce specialty books such as cookbooks or calendars. Blurb

Website Tip: Add dynamic content to a blog. Comments, Online Search, News Feeds, Site Search, Pictures, to name a few, can be added to attract interest. A wide range of dynamic contact is offered by blog-publishing services and can be easily formatted into the sidebars of any blog. To draw a visitor's attention to any specific area, use a bright, large font.

Marketing Tip: Start a topical group on Yahoo or Google groups. If the group grows and you are prepared to produce helpful information on a timely basis, consider sending out newsletters. Here's an excellent tutorial on turning a G-mail post into a template for a mini Newsletter. <u>Video</u>

Week Thirty-Three

Dream in a pragmatic way.
– Aldous Huxley

Writing Tip: A word about empathy. Artists must understand, feel, be open to, the experience of humankind. Otherwise how can their creative work have meaning to the audience who listens, watches or reads? For some artists the ability to take on different personas is natural. For others, it's a trait that must be honed. Opportunities to develop empathy are everywhere. When conflict arises in your world, imagine taking the perspective of the other. A better person and better writer awaits.

Editing Tip: Profanity comes in many forms. Essentially, it's offensive language about God, sex, bodily functions, men, women, race, religion, to name a few. So how much profanity is too much? And where's the line? If you're a publishing writer, no one's going to stop you from using whatever language you want, but how many readers are you willing to turn off in the process? My advice: save yourself the aggravation and only use profanity when it really, really matters.

Publishing Tip: Publishing an e-book for a Kindle is done through Amazon's Kindle Direct Publishing. The process is straightforward and relatively easy. One must upload a .jpg cover and Word document preferably saved as a simple web page. Before publication, a writer can see how the book will read on a Kindle and edit it accordingly. Every author sets the cover price. For books priced between $2.99 and $9.99, the writer gets a 70% royalty. Besides this caveat of pricing, writers must also agree to allow the text-to-speech and book-lending options. Otherwise the royalty rate is 35%. Kindle pays only when an e-book is sold. Edits can be made at anytime at no cost. KDP

Website Tip: To beef up credibility on your website, include text and hyperlinks (clickable links) that savvy visitors may be interested in. As an example, if your book is a police procedural, mention Evan Hunter (a writer who is credited with inventing the genre) then put a clickable link to his bio or some interesting tidbit. Designate that the link open in a new page so when the link is closed, your website will reappear.

Marketing Tip: Who's your audience? Be specific. And where do they lurk? Defining an audience is not difficult, but taking the time to come up with a plan of reaching them is often overlooked. After writing and editing and publishing, forgetting this one step can easily be lost in the many endless tasks. Focused marketing is the best use of your time. Curiously, I was very focused with my first book, *Rented Rooms,* but then got off track with my second book, *Paloma*. I saw this novel as part mystery, part suspense, part romance, part latina, part for older readers, part this, part that, on and on. Looking back, the better way to have marketed this book was to play to a specific audience. These are the questions I should have asked myself... What is *Paloma*? A mystery. What kind of mystery? Contemporary with a romantic element. And what other author writes similarly? Nora Roberts. And where are her readers? With each question, zero in, then devise a plan. Only when concerted efforts fail, should another campaign be started. Defining a book as a book for all seasons, will spread your marketing initiative too thin. The result: spotty sales.

Week Thirty-Four

If you see the magic in a fairy tale, you can face the future.
– Danielle Steel

Writing Tip: Twists in a story can happen in small and large ways. Good storytelling is a fine balancing act, an interplay of what is known and not known, what is familiar and not familiar. The more you can surprise the reader, the more he'll be delighted. When a character reacts to a situation, event, conversation, give yourself some options beyond the expected. For instance...a man gets a Dear John letter, how does he respond? with blubbering tears or hysterical laughter? Yes, the event could throw him into a deep depression but perhaps his first reaction is that's she's joking, looking for attention. Like he'd fall for that one. Ha Ha.

Editing Tip: Even though there are many characters in a book, they are created from one mind. Naturally, characters can be differentiated in how they behave and dress, but how about their speech? Years ago there was a recurrent Saturday Night Live skit where two women from public television rambled on in stereo monotone. Amusing, but not for print. Speech can be differentiated by manner and the language used. Is your character hesitant, loquacious, laconic? Does an aging professor use slang? a ten-year old talk about metaphysics? Whatever the case, have each character's speech mirror who they are.

Publishing Tip: Having your picture on or inside a book or website or blog is fairly standard. I never thought it was important until a reader commented to me that an author's picture helped him decide whether or not to buy the book. I can't say that's a deal breaker for me, but I do look at authors' pictures. Recently, I've noticed a preponderance of hats. Many others are smiling or staring off. Some are snapshots, others high-end portraits. The bit of advice I offer is to make sure your picture remains proportional. In other words, when a photograph is resized, keep the aspect ratio intact. This will avoid funhouse mutations.

Website Tip: In deciding on a host service, find out if they offer unlimited domains or at least a few for the same cost as one domain. Having this option allows for growth. Who knows where your writing and publishing will lead. I know my journey has been a surprise every step of the way. While other URL names will have to be rented for a nominal fee, having multiple domains (one with your book name, another with your name, perhaps a third with a totally different slant or interest) allows you to spread out and beef-up your presence on the web. Keep in mind, every URL should be updated regularly to keep traffic coming.

Marketing Tip: Sell books on the secondary market at Amazon. This page shows up when you click *used* or *other buying choices.* There's no restriction from authors selling books on either their book page or the secondary market. Either way Amazon makes money. To snag sales, identify yourself as the author and offer an autographed book. Place this info under *seller information*. If you choose to price the book competitively, don't go below the lowest price. This could start a low-ball bidding war between yourself and another seller.

Week Thirty-Five
The road to hell is paved with works-in-progress.
– Philip Roth

Writing Tip: The showdown or climax of your story is the do-or-die scene for your protagonist. The sooner you know the who, what, when, where, how of this scene, the better you'll be able to plan and shoot for it. In fact, endings and beginnings can grow from this event alone. The showdown scene is dire straits, an all-or-nothing scenario. Impending death always builds suspense or that last meeting between a lover, parent, friend. On the other hand, a climatic scene with little or no conse-quences (Will Lola be admitted to Harvard?) may be a lot harder to pull off.

Editing Tip: Phrases or punctuation that shout "Look at me" need to be cut. Some attention-seeking hogs...Exclamation points. Only place them in dialogue and even then sparingly. Let the language do the shout-ing. Italics. When used to accentuate – like *he* ever cared – is an overused device that makes writing hi-strionic. Description or metaphors that cut into the mood. In other words, avoid describing the way the rain falls when your protagonist is drowning in an undercur-rent and has immediate matters to attend to.

Publishing Tip: Subtitles matter, especially since searching keywords is what the Internet (and finding a book) is all about. When coming up with a subtitle utilize a keyword search tool, then place those commonly used keywords in an order that flows. To get a feel for sub-titles, check out successful books. Rather than having named by first novel: *Paloma,* I could have called it, *Pa-loma: A Novel*, or better still, Paloma: *A Latina Mystery*, or perhaps, *Paloma: A Mystery of a Latina with Three Identities.* Subtitles aren't used every time a book is identified. Titles still reign supreme in that area. Still, adding a subtitle attracts attention, gives it a searchable/marketable edge, and distinguishes your book from others with the same title. Keyword

Website Tip: Web builders have everything needed to design a website, but free add-on elements for fonts, logos, buttons, can also be placed into your site. Cool Text

Marketing Tip: Register your book with BookCrossing, get a code, and send it into the wild. An ingenious program that started years ago, Book- Crossing had the idea of making the world an open library. Once coded, your book, or any other book you wish to share, is left somewhere for others to pick up, read, then pass along. If the book is marked with an identifying number and a reader is so inclined, he can return to the site and comment about the book. BookCrossing

Week Thirty-Six

I always say ideas are like fishing.
– David Lynch

Writing Tip: An opening scene should introduce the main character, present her dilemma and begin the forward trajectory by placing her off balance. Where and how a story opens is critical, because that's when the reader gets hooked. No matter what kind of story you're telling – mystery, romance, sci-fi, literary – the first sentence, paragraph, and page must have punch in clarity, tone, emotion, and conflict. There's no warming up, no meandering allowed. Ditto for nonfiction as journalists know well.

Editing Tip: Read work aloud to get a sense of the rhythm of the language. At which points do you naturally stop or move ahead full steam? Does punctuation – commas and periods – reflect the cadence? Are there places where you stumble, where the fluidness of the language breaks up? Do you say a different word than is written? These are all telltale signs where some tweaking may be warranted. Akin to reading aloud, is taping yourself for playback.

Publishing Tip: Pre-printed covers have an edge around them that are called "bleeds". These bleeds are areas where books are trimmed. A bleed must not have any elements that are important: text, ISBN number or images you want seen. The bleed for all book covers is .6 cm (.25 inch) for the height and .3 cm (.125 inch) for the width. There are no bleeds for the edge that runs along the spine (that which connects the front and back cover).

Website Tip: Grab a visitor's immediate attention with a headline. Headlines that draw visitors can be in the form of a question, a how-to promise, an interesting quote, a topical news announcement, an enlightening fact. Once the headline is written, the next trick is to write an equally interesting follow-up that addresses and expands upon the headline. Nonfiction books are naturals for headline material. Fiction books can be made to fit. Headline: *"Love's complicated," Paloma says*. Followed by: *She knows first hand. Twenty-five years and Max still hovers.*

Marketing Tip: Books for Soldiers is a program that sends books to our troops. The process involves some paperwork but is a great way to promote your book and find several readers. A book sent to one soldier is sure to be passed around. <u>Books for Soldiers</u>

Week Thirty-Seven

If you can't annoy somebody, there's little point in writing.
– Kingsley Amis

Writing Tip: Before the last words are written tie up loose ends, resolve subplots, show us how the protagonist has changed, and illustrate how human nature with all its foibles continues. Often times readers remember what they last read. For this reason, an ending can be powerful. Endings don't necessarily have to be happy. Bittersweet works, as does a hard lesson learned. Perhaps the only ill-advised ending is to kill off the protagonist, something I had considered until a dear friend threw the manuscript at me.

Editing Tip: As counterpoint to the tip above, a quote from Raymond Chandler: *The ideal mystery is one you would read if the end was missing.* I feel this holds true no matter the genre. The true test of a great story is if it captures a reader's attention moment by moment. A tall order to be sure but doable. In the editing process, look for dead spots, not just the minutiae of boring words, phrases, description, etc., but pages, that if removed, don't affect the storyline, don't prompt change, don't show emotion.

Publishing Tip: When books are ordered for resale, check them out. Have any been damaged in the shipping process? Are the books bound upside down? Did you receive the number ordered? Scan the interior. Is the type clear? Does the book appear to have the correct number of pages? If an updated edition, have the proper changes been made? I've personally experienced all of the above problems with either my books or ones I've purchased from bookstores, which leads me to conclude these are not isolated events.

Website Tip: The *About Us* web page, or in the case of an author, the *About Me* web page is an opportunity to establish rapport with a reader. Some tips: say a few words about yourself; include a picture; pass along some interesting unique information about your book: why you wrote it, why you're passionate about it; encourage the reader to contact you with any questions; provide an e-mail link on the page.

Marketing Tip: Selling to libraries crosses every writer's mind. Some pointers to access this market are…Write a book that appears library worthy, that is to say, a unique but topical nonfiction book that is well-researched, and has 1. an index, 2. Library of Congress Cataloguing-in-Publication block, 3. a subject tag on the back cover, 4. been reviewed by the Library Journal. For placing your book in the local library, you may only have to contact the acquisition librarian. Another path to library sales is to suggest a program or class on the topic of your book. Should this get you in the door, magic may follow.

Week Thirty-Eight
Obviously, a writer can't know everything about what she writes. It's impossible.
– Anne Rice

Writing Tip: Avoid down time by carrying a journal for ideas, a book to read, or your own work to edit. Productivity and progress can be made in snippets of time throughout the day.

Editing Tip: After years of editing, you're sure to have an idea of certain recurrent propensities toward copy written poorly. Complicated sentences, the overuse of *look*, a tendency to over describe are some of mine. Keep a log of your writing sins so that you'll be reminded to edit them. Eventually, and with mindfulness, these tiresome edits will self correct during the writing process.

Publishing Tip: Choosing a text font. Options: serif and sans-serif. Serif is any font that has tags attached to the letters such as: Times New Roman, Garamond. Sans-serif fonts with no such no tags are: Arial or Verdana (used in this book). Serif is more widely used in book printing, while sans-serif is used on the Internet. Whatever your preference, make sure the font is easy to read. Specialty fonts are better suited for titles than text.

Website Tip: Cascading Style Sheets (CSS) is a website language that lays out HTML elements. Essentially, CSS formats document presentation as opposed to document content. The advantage of CSS is that many pages can be changed at once, in other words, macro changes can be executed. CSS is not saved in the web page itself but in a .css file that is then referred to by a code that is placed in the web page. There are tutorials to learn about CSS. CSS

Marketing Tip: To set up a <u>FaceBook Fan Page</u>, go to FaceBook Fan Page, select product/brand, enter title, click *Get Started*. Follow the prompts to *Open Facebook* account, add image, invite friends, import contacts, add *website*, add *about you*, click, and your page will appear. Fan Pages can be for individual books or authors.

Week Thirty-Nine

*There is no such thing as a great talent
without great will power.*
– Honore de Balzac

Writing Tip: Most stories are written in the simple past
– *he ran, I thought, she wished* – even though the story
action is happening in the present. At first this may
seem jarring but with practice, the use of past tense be-
comes second nature. Tenses, generally, should not be
mixed. I suspect this happens because we often use
multiple tenses in our daily lives. Personally, I enjoy the
freshness of the present tense, but this can be problematic. Readers have expectations in how a story is told.
To keep the waters calm, stick with the tense that pre-
vails for that genre.

Editing Tip: To slow the pace while editing for minutiae,
tap each word with your finger/pencil or use another
piece of paper to cover the lines below the line you are
reading. This technique also helps to avoid skimming the
text.

Publishing Tip: If you make your publishing company
as an LLC, you may have to provide Affidavits of Publication. Affidavits are public notices of formation in the
classified ad section in newspapers. In New York State,
ads can only be placed in certain papers, for a certain
length of time, and must have specific information. To
make sure you are doing everything correctly, contact
the county clerk, and format the ad similar to others
found in the classified section. Once properly published,
the newspaper will issue affidavits that are then submitted to the state. Affidavits must be published and submitted to the state in a timely fashion.

Website Tip: Many hosts offer access to raw web server logs. These logs give more specific information on a

website's traffic than a regular statistics program. Pouring over this info can be helpful in fine tuning your website and marketing tactics. In some cases, to view the logs you must do two things: download the log into your computer and utilize a log analyzer program to pull out and present the data. There is no cost to doing this. Look inside your panel to see how to save the log to your computer, then download a free web analyzer. Should a Perl Interpreter be needed for the analyzer to do its job, a link should appear when the program is executed. Analyzer Log

Marketing Tip: With the fluidity of e-publishing, one can price an e-book for free for any length of time. Free books draw readers. Pricing free books is easily done if your books are being distributed by Smashwords. One click and the free price will go into effect for as long or short, as you like. Kindle (except for their Select program) does not allow books priced below .99. However, they will match a book price found on other sites. To make a book free on Kindle, once that same book has a zero price on another site, alert Amazon by going to that book's Amazon page and, under Product Details, click *tell us about a lower price*.

Week Forty

Don't live down to expectations.
Go out and do something remarkable.
– Wendy Wasserstein

Writing Tip: Whenever you're stuck for ideas, brainstorm, and ask yourself a question about the situation/scene your protagonist is in. A simple query could be about what he sees. A more abstract question could be what he thinks or feels. Write the question down, then answer with the possibilities that come to mind. After a list is developed, zero in on those ideas that intrigue you. The process of brainstorming is fun, expansive, associative, and can be utilized at every level of storytelling.

Editing Tip: Edit body of work separate from headings. Headings appear in contents, chapter titles, and in the back matter such as the glossary or index. Besides spelling, look at the font, and spacing both in the title itself and its position on the page. When changes are made to the body of the manuscript, the pagination of a chapter beginning may also change. If you are preparing the manuscript for publication, add referring pages numbers to contents and/or index after all changes have been made to the final, formatted file that goes to the printer. If a subsidy is publishing your manuscript, they will attach the referring page numbers. Once the final galley is received, the listed page numbers should be reviewed carefully.

Publishing Tip: A reprint is a print book that has minor changes such as price or corrected typos. A reprint does not require a new ISBN. A new edition is a book that is substantially changed, expanded upon or shortened. A new edition receives a new copyright and printing date. A different ISBN is required for the following substantive changes: a new title/publisher; a binding change, i.e., hardcover to paperback.

Website Tip: Free web add-ons are available for any website. Many are interactive and can increase return visitors. Others are just fun. Here's a short list: counter, calendar, guestbook, headline news, site search, chat room, survey, mailing list, message forum. When you consider what to place on your site, be selective. What are your needs? How do you want to be perceived? Are you prepared to maintain whatever you start? Bravenet (Also includes ways to build newsletter, e-mail templates.)

Marketing Tip: Give reasons why readers should read your book and place these reasons in a list format that can be scanned quickly and easily. To devise a list, think of your audience. Is the book of a certain genre? What other author might a potential reader also like? Does the story take place during a certain time? What can a reader learn? What is the underlying theme of the book?

Week Forty-One
Always do what you are afraid to do.
– Ralph Waldo Emerson

Writing Tip: Increase writing prowess by exploring other writing formats. Read poetry for language, plays for dialogue, screenplays for description snippets, newspapers for directness, novels for storytelling, short fiction for tight prose.

Editing Tip: Suggested bedside reading: *Chicago Manual of Style* (University of Chicago Press Staff) and/or *The Elements of Style* (Strunk). Not only references, both these books can be, in brief segments and depending on your quirkiness, fun and instructive.

Publishing Tip: When you are your own publisher, timely book sale information is accessible from your account be it with Amazon, Apple, Smashwords, Lightning Source, etc. If, on the other hand, you are not the primary publisher but are being published by a subsidy or commercial publisher, some sales info can be found at NovelRank (Amazon) and BookChart (Apple).

Website Tip: Zeroing in on single words and short phrases can make the difference between a good site and a great site. Attracting words like *Free offer*, *Discount*, *Sale*, *Free trial*, *Try us out*, are powerful action-generating words that snag interest. For a book site this could refer to an excerpt, free download, or book sale. Headline and body text should repeat keywords and targeted words that are in your meta tags. Persuasive words, as opposed to bragging words, can come from clips of reviews you've received. Highlight words in bright contrasting colors.

Marketing Tip: Book Trailers are easy to design and can be done for free. The trick is to make the trailer interesting, unique, funny or something that will grab a reader's interest, and if truly remarkable, go viral. Watch the good ones (tons on YouTube) to get an idea. Trailers can be placed everywhere. <u>Animoto</u> <u>Xtranormal</u>

Week Forty-Two
I wish I could write as mysterious as a cat.
– Edgar Allan Poe

Writing Tip: Characters in a novel or story should be actively for or against your protagonist. Keeping this in mind gives that pro or con character purpose, motivation, and provides a vehicle for tension. Should a named character be neutral in his relationship with the protagonist, his minor, ineffective role should be cut before he co-opts the integrity of the story.

Editing Tip: Words to search and evaluate for deletion are adverbs (*ly* endings) and participles (*ing* endings). In many cases adverbs modify weak, overused or vague verbs, i.e., *he spoke loudly.* Whenever an adverb crops up, try making the verb stronger, i.e., *he bellowed*. Participles are verbs often used at the beginning of a sentence. Problems occur when the subject to this verb is missing, not placed properly, or when the action described doesn't make sense in context. Respective examples: *Walking down the street, a car swerved around the corner.* Who's walking down the street? The car? *Running down the hall, Marie was surprised to see Rover loose.* Subject (Rover) is too removed from the modifying participle. *Jumping from the chair*, *Carol answered the door.* Sounds like Carol's jumping and answering the door at the same time.

Publishing Tip: CreateSpace is a Print-on-Demand Amazon program that publishes print books at no or low upfront cost. Advantages: an ISBN number is provided; author copies can be purchased at the most competitive rates; authors receive a sixty percent royalty rate for books sold from Amazon.com; a proof copy (nominal cost) is available prior to publication; built-in, worldwide distribution; customer support. All pre-publication tasks: editing, cover design/layout, manuscript formatting, must be undertaken by the author. If an author needs help, fee-services are available. <u>CreateSpace</u>

Website Tip: Expand keywords by adding plurals and using different forms of important words, i.e., police procedural, police stories, cop mystery, officers on the beat. As a reminder, these same keywords should also be placed in the website's content.

Marketing Tip: Just like a writer's group can help your writing, a book marketing group is a tremendous resource for publishing writers. Joining or starting a marketing group where you live is especially helpful since local venues provide direct access to a buying base. Besides providing support, members of a book marketing group can share resources, outlets, contacts, and mistakes to avoid.

Week Forty-Three
The violets in the mountains have broken the rocks.
– Tennessee Williams

Writing Tip: For the most bang, villains, those characters we love to hate, should be ruthless and determined. Of course, they can be charming and clever and good-looking as well. Depending on the kind of story, antagonists may have many shades: an overbearing mother could be the go-to-gal for arranging potluck fundraisers; the fire-starting pastor, a great orator on the pulpit. A second type of villain could be a bank, a bear, a blizzard. For these types of bad guys to work, human characteristics must be assigned to them. Yet another villain may be the protagonist herself as she wrangles internal demons. But since this type of internal conflict should occur in every story, an external villain is always welcomed.

Editing Tip: Lists of any kind should be evaluated. They are especially tiresome in fiction: *Peonies, tulips, English ivy, roses, pumpkins, and an old tire filled the garden.* Better to have your mind's eye focus on one tulip, its color, texture, position; the way the light hits, petals spread. Detail is always more vivid than general references.

Publishing Tip: Smashwords is an e-book publisher and distributor. A writer can submit his work, put it through Smashwords's meatgrinder (their formatting machine), then place it into distribution (Nook, Apple, Sony Reader, Diesel, and more) for free. Smashwords also: allows you to place free books on their site; provides free ISBNs; gives you the choice to opt out of any distribution channel; allows authors to set the cover price; and pays the hightest royalty (85%) for books sold from their site. Smashwords (At this time, Smashwords does not distribute to Kindle.)

Website Tip: Certain problems that adversely affect a spider's ability to crawl your site, that then can negatively impact your website's ranking, are: having a server that is inaccessible; duplicate title/meta tags/content on different pages of the site; overuse of targeted keywords (stuffing); failure to update site often.

Marketing Tip: Dress a sales table with: a cloth (a sheet's fine), books on easels, promotional material, and if outside, paperweights (stones work great). Bring change, calculator, and a comfortable light-weight folding chair (mine's got an umbrella too). Carry books inside a wheeled suitcase or granny's wire shopping cart.

Week Forty-Four

The secret of getting ahead is getting started.
– Agatha Christie

Writing Tip: What makes a story worth telling? The answer lies within you, the author. A story worth telling is one that drives you, quickens your pulse, keeps you up at night. If the passion's not there in the beginning, that story isn't yours to tell. After that, it's a matter of staying loose, spontaneous and refusing to be sabotaged by inhibition and self doubt.

Editing Tip: Nouns. Are they specific, vivid, concrete? A human is vague, a man is less vague, a robust, red-faced college kid in a wrinkled tux is spot on. I see him right now. Don't give him another drink.

Publishing Tip: <u>Lightning Source</u> is the company that prints POD books for the publishing industry. They only service publishers, not individual writers. However, should an author become a publisher, he can access the benefits of Lightning Source. So how does a writer become a publisher? By having a bank of ISBN numbers (at this time, ten numbers cost around $300) in his publishing company's name. That's all. Of course that just gets you in the door. Besides the cost of ISBNs, software to convert final documents and covers into PDF files are needed. If you choose to incorporate that's an additional expense. Still, these expenses buy a ton of freedom and control. Advantages: The cost to publish is around $75. Author copies are price without any middleman charges. Distribution is worldwide. Trade discount is at your discretion. There are no royalty splits. Disadvantages: No handholding. A writer/publisher must take on every aspect of writing, publishing, marketing plus stay current with those changes that affect the process.

Website Tip: Blogs, like websites, can be submitted to directories, search engines and feed syndication sites. Blog Directories Blog on Blogging

Marketing Tip: High concept is a term used in filmmaking that refers to a storyline summarized in a couple of sentences. When selling in person, a high concept presentation for each book is extremely helpful. Hone the plot to an intriguing sentence or two and you'll be armed and ready to make a sale when a visitor scurries by.

Week Forty-Five
Failure is the condiment that gives success its flavor.
– Truman Capote

Writing Tip: When to summarize or when to tell the story in moment by moment action? Summary should be used when there is no or little emotional content. This could be background, description, or any information that is told rather than shown. Action scenes, on the other hand, focus on feelings, not in broad strokes but in moment by moment rising drama.

Editing Tip: Should a slew of sentences have pronouns, a closer look is warranted. Example: *I've written eight books. My books are fiction and nonfiction. I've been writing for almost twenty years. It's been quite a journey, but I've managed to get this far.* Rewrite: *After a twenty-year journey, I've managed to write eight books, three fiction and two nonfiction.*

Publishing Tip: Before Print-on-Demand technology and e-books, self-publishing was restricted to those brave souls who contacted a printer and bulk ordered books. It was a huge investment. However, times have changed and today anyone can publish for no money at all. Yes. Free publishing. And everyone's on the bandwagon. If you've written a paper for school, a report for work, or just about anything on any topic of any length, e-publishing is now available. It's simply a matter of having a computer to format your work then uploading it to a multitude of sites. You can charge for data download or give it away for free. It can be an advertising tool or a budding publishing business. Many may scoff, that publishing electronically is not real publishing. Tell that to the booming e-reader business and readers who will never buy a book again. Here are some sites where you can publish for free: <u>Amazon's Kindle</u>, <u>Lulu</u>, <u>Smashwords</u>, <u>Feedbooks</u>.

Website Tip: Your statistics output should indicate where your visitors are coming from, i.e., search engines, directories or other sites. Reviewing referrer information lets you know if your site is indexed and ranked high on a particular search engine. When visitors come to your site via a search engine, you can assume your site is indexed and ranked fairly high. Conversely, after 2-3 months, the lack of search engine referrals may suggest your site is not indexed in their database or not ranked high enough. (Week Forty-Seven)

Marketing Tip: Natural places to sell books are at book fairs. They're all over the country and readers flock to them. However, the cost of gas, accommodations and set-up fees can be expensive. Competition is also a factor. Publishing houses show up with freebies and star authors who give talks and sign books. Still, fairs are fun and a good way to work the crowd and get your name out there. Expenses can be pared down if you attend with other writers or offer to display their titles. Giving presentations can also capture a throng's attention. Book Fairs

Week Forty-Six

*The cleverest of all, in my opinion, is the man
who calls himself a fool at least once a month.*
– Fyodor Dostoevsky

Writing Tip: Sex-scene pointers for mainstream, commercial stories: know your audience and their expectations; have the scene move the plot forward; use five senses; incorporate small telling details; build tension. Avoid the following: medical/derogatory terms; questionable metaphors (*cherry pit nipples*); euphemisms (*heading for home base*); cliché dialogue ("*Make me a woman. Oh baby. Oh baby.*") An exception to the above is erotica thin on storyline.

Editing Tip: Fewer is used when an item can be counted; less is used when it can't be counted, i.e., less money but fewer dollar bills; less time but fewer minutes.

Publishing Tip: A collection of work is by one author. An anthology is the work of many authors. Anthologies are put together by editors who in turn are contracted with publishers. When putting together an anthology, editors must secure permissions from contributors. Such permissions also stipulate what rights are being transferred. This usually includes one- time rights and/or electronic rights should the author's work or part of the work be used for advertising purposes. Permissions should also address elements commonly found in publishing contracts, i.e., payment, when work is expected to be published, when rights revert to author, etc.

Website Tip: Just as you advertise your book, advertise your website. Place your URL on all promotional materials: business cards, flyers, press releases, bookmarks. Also include your website in all signatures: e-mail, articles, forums, blogs. Some knowledge of HTML may be

needed when the simple URL address doesn't automatically link to your site. Usually sites have directions with how to format your signature. If you can't figure it out, contact the site. To give you an idea of how a signature can be formatted as:
HTML:[url=http://www.yoursite.com/]Title of Book[/url]
This would read as a hyperlink named Title of Book, that when clicked would go to your website. HTML

Marketing Tip: Selling foreign rights can be lucrative because the same book can be sold to many markets. Can be done through an agent or on your own. Steps: Research foreign agents who are looking for material, send along a book summary, trailer, link to website/book page. If interest follows, forward a foreign rights packet that includes a book and detailed summary of the book's uniqueness, marketability, and sales history.

Week Forty-Seven
Talking, talking. Spinning a web of words,
pale walls of dreams, between myself and all I see.
– John Gardner

Writing Tip: Readers of category (western, romance, mystery, sci-fi, fantasy, literary, young adult, historical, to name some) have expectations. Such readers are also extremely knowledgeable. The best way to capture their interest is to provide them with a unique read within their comfort level. Some writers chase markets. *The DaVinci Code* is written and suddenly all kinds of writers are immersed in their version of *The DaVinci Code II*. Not a particular problem in itself, but to pull this off, the writer needs to be aware of the nuances of writing this type of mystery, be able to research, then make the story fresh. An especially tall order if you write fantasy and not mystery.

Editing Tip: The subjunctive case expresses a wish, possibility or a hypothetical scenario that isn't a fact. The subjunctive case is often used after *if*, *as if*, *as though*, *unless*. The subjunctive of the verb *to be* is *were*. *If I were you, I'd pay the ticket.* Subjunctives aren't always used in informal writing or speech, but they're still important to understand and utilize when necessary.

Publishing Tip: The more money you spend to publish your book, the more you'll have to sell to make a profit. Given the options, there is absolutely no need to spend a lot of money to get your book published. However, an honest evaluation of your strengths and weaknesses should be made in your ability to create a book. Are you able to design a cover? Edit? Prepare the book for printing? Money saved in one area can be spent in another. To get the most bang for the buck, consider all book publishing choices, network with other writers, and be

willing to learn and expand those skills needed to publish. Should you intend to publish multiple books, every
bit of knowledge learned will pay back tenfold.

Website Tip: It may take weeks or months to get fully
on board with the search engines and directories. You'll
get a sense of progress from your statistics page where
search engine visits and/or robot/spider visits are docu-
mented. In the meantime, keep updating pages with interesting and unique content. Every couple of months,
resubmit your site to search engines, both small and
large. With time, you should notice higher placement
and more visitors.

Marketing Tip: To sell on eBay consider the following:
single books sell better than advertising a number of
them; include a picture of the book and a comprehensive description; special interest, hobby books do well;
tap into a wider customer base by placing the book in
different categories, i.e., *Weekly Strategies for Writers*
could be auctioned in Reference, Hobbies and Crafts,
Teaching and Education, Others. eBay

Week Forty-Eight
It's like driving a car at night. You never see further than your headlights, but you can make the whole trip that way.
– E. L. Doctorow

Writing Tip: Passive, indecisive, boring characters bleed the life out of a story. Make supporting characters feisty, obsessive, assertive and, when possible, desirous of certain outcomes that conflict with those of your protagonist. This will turn up the heat on our poor leading lady or man who is, by design, also living on the edge.

Editing Tip: A nonfiction book should look like one. Inclusions to consider are: an index, glossary, bibliography, appendices. On the back cover place a subject line. Adding these elements is easy and makes your book reference-friendly. Reviewers also look for these little extras that demonstrate professionalism. To see how other books arrange these elements, go to either Google Books or Amazon's SearchInside and preview books similar to yours.

Publishing Tip: Offset printing is publishing bulk book orders by going to a book printing company where the book is printed using an offset printer. Advantages: the lowest unit cost per book; little technical knowledge other than following the submission guidelines; depending on the company, some frills – provision of ISBN and/or editing services – can be ordered with publication. Disadvantages: high start up cost due to the number of books that must be initially ordered; book storage issues; no built-in distribution; edits can only be made on new bulk orders; not all printers print books; printing company may not be local. Offset is a good option for a niche book that can be sold in your locality.

Website Tip: Website statistics show both page views

(clicks to HTML pages) and hits (landings to server). Hits far outnumber page views since they are counted by hitting on the page and whatever server links are on that page, i.e., images or CSS files. For instance, if you have five images on a home page and a visitor clicks onto the page, the stats will show one page view and six hits (one to the page and one to each image that is saved in the server.) In evaluating your statistics, page views are more important than hits. The more pages a visitor views, the better. This factor is called "stickiness" and means your content is keeping visitors on the site. Conversely, a visitor who alights onto a page then quickly clicks off may indicate that some tweaking to content is needed.

Marketing Tip: Webinars enable speakers to give seminars, along with screen shots, via a computer. They can be set up on a regular basis or one-time only. Webinars can also be recorded, saved, and played at another time. Usually a webinar consists of a topic presentation followed by Q&A. Like any talk, plan your content and speak slowly and clearly. AnyMeeting

Week Forty-Nine

Tell me and I forget. Teach me and I remember.
Involve me and I learn.
– Benjamin Franklin

Writing Tip: Write, don't tell the whole story. Having an idea for a story is very exciting. So exciting (and may I add brilliant) you may want to share, chapter and verse, the entire yarn. This is not a good idea. First, you may be greeted with a less than enthusiastic response that in turn will leave you wilted and ashamed. Secondly, telling the story dissipates passion so that when you sit down to write the process feels more like a tiresome rehash than a creative journey. Not a good way to spend precious waking hours.

Editing Tip: Compound words can be open (cross section), closed (catlike) or hyphenated (full-length). And it's a fluid situation. Is it nonfiction or non-fiction? Self published or self-published? In some cases a definitive, agreed-upon answer can't be found and the best way to spell compound words is to simply be consistent throughout the work. To learn a bevy of mind-bending rules check out *The Chicago Manual of Style*.

Publishing Tip: Making your own book. I've seen many creative books that are either homemade or sent to the local printer to be copied and bound. Some examples: a plastic-comb bound cookbook with regional recipes, a calendar-style pictorial book on the Erie Canal, poetry books folded portrait length and stapled. When done well and with the proper audience, these books can be produced inexpensively and sold for significant profit. Since these books rarely have ISBNs, make sure you place contact information on the cover.

Website Tip: Statistic programs monitor visitors to each page on your website. Should some pages dominate visitor interest, think about ways to draw the visitor from the popular page to the less popular page. Perhaps a special offer or an interesting link will draw attention. If the page remains anemic, it may need to be retooled with new content.

Marketing Tip: Twitter basics: find and follow people whose topics are of mutual interest; when posting include a link back to you (website, book page), shorten URLs with <u>Bitly,</u> do giveaways, provide information, post questions.

Week Fifty

I have no particular talent. I am merely inquisitive.
– Albert Einstein

Writing Tip: Make your hero, well, heroic. Bravery is a trait we all admire, a trait that is threaded in most stories told. Why so? It mirrors our lives, or at least our ideal lives, those people who we want to be. Danger, the unknown, fear are all situations common to humanity, but at times our responses to adversity are less than courageous. Still, that doesn't mean we don't try. A hero who faces tremendous odds reflects our own struggles. And when he rises to the occasion, we, as readers, rise with him.

Editing Tip: Question marks. Besides their use at the end of a query, question marks can be used within sentences, after questioning elements, i.e., *What for? and why today? he wondered.* On the other hand an indirect question does not use a question mark, i.e., *He asked if we had food in the house.*

Publishing Tip: Besides Amazon's CreateSpace for print books and Kindle for e-books, Amazon has other publishing programs worthy of note: Kindle Select and Kindle Single. First, it is important to understand that both these digital (not print) publishing options are exclusive, meaning you can not e-publish the piece anywhere else on the Internet. However, there is an advantage to each. With <u>Kindle Select</u>, an author can make his e-book free (a great form of advertising) for up to five days every 3 months. With <u>Kindle Single</u>, once accepted into the program, an author is able to price an e-book below $2.99 and still get the full 70% royalty.

Website Tip: Google offers links to check your site. To see if your site is listed with Google, type this into your browser:

http://www.google.com/search?q=YRURL+site:www.YR
URL To find the backlinks that point to your URL, type
this in your browser:
http://www.google.com/search?as_lq=YRURL
(Note: YRURL field refers to your website name.)

Marketing Tip: Local events can be found in local papers, including Pennysavers, Bees, and any number of
free weeklies put out by communities. Similar listings
are found online in local hubs and classifieds. Keep an
eye out for venues where books can be sold. Also look
for places where there is less competition (fewer booksellers) AND where your book will cost less than what's
being sold.

Week Fifty-One

Publication is a self-invasion of privacy.
– Marshall McLuhan

Writing Tip: Transparency is a common buzz word that denotes clarity, the ability to be seen through. Great actors have this gift. When they perform, who they are in real life seeps into the background and a new persona shines through. In many ways every artist strives for this: to be pure expression separate from him or herself. Writers are no different. To achieve transparency, keep your ego at bay by avoiding: an agenda thinly disguised; haughty words meant to impress; any other egocentric ramblings that point to you and only you.

Editing Tip: Editing is not writing more. Editing is evaluating, cutting, honing, tightening, polishing. If you're "editing" a 100K manuscript and ending up with a 150K manuscript you're still writing – not editing – as well as adding copy that will need editing. Editing is less of an art than writing but still demands enormous skill. Left-brained and analytical, editing is precise and no nonsense. We hate to cut words, sentences, paragraphs, pages, chapters. We worked so hard on that clever obscure phrase, that insightful repetitive interior thought, that runaway scene of pure inspiration. Sorry. They got to go.

Publishing Tip: Publishing a first book is a lot of work. There's much to learn. Still, some thought should be made to branding. Branding is used in advertising to grab attention and associate a product with a company. Besides words, branding can include logos, colors, images, music, and the like. With only one book, you may not consider this important, but this is where branding begins. Branding, done well and early, paves the way for product identification. It's not necessary to have an entire campaign up and running, but consider some basic elements – a logo, a saying, a book cover – that can be built upon.

Website Tip: Templates make website design easy. To personalize a template you can: add a logo, header; change the pictures; customize the background by adding textures or a different color; change the navigation links; vary the script. When looking at templates, consider the basic layout. Do you want three columns? Or a couple of blocks on the right or left margins? Look at other sites and see what catches your eye. You can do a lot with a standard layout that has a wide center column with two narrower columns flanking each side.

Marketing Tip: Selling books doesn't preclude selling other items. Photographs, bookmarks, how-to brochures, CDs, or anything else germane to your book or books in general can be offered. If selling in person, you may even offer inexpensive non-book items to draw people to your table. While ideas can be found at every cash register check-out, keep in mind you want to attract book buyers. For instance, selling jewelry with books could become problematic should jewelry customers plant themselves at your display thereby blocking potential book buyers.

Week Fifty-Two

There is wisdom of the head, and wisdom of the heart.
– Charles Dickens

Writing Tip: Every moment you write, progress is made. There may be mistakes, tangential side trips, and points where giving up seems the only option. Learning any task is done in progressive stages. But those stages are different for each of us. One person's strength is another's weakness. Right-brained, imaginative, subjective concepts are not so easily defined or taught especially when there's negative inside chatter. Be kind to yourself and pop a cork for every success be it a finished chapter or book.

Editing Tip: Should you do your own editing? Many writers emphatically say – no. However, should this task be farmed out you won't learn much and you'll probably keep making the same mistakes. I believe every publishing writer needs to make the manuscript as flawless as possible, then possibly head over to an editor. For my novel I had a professional editor (one with credits) do what he called a diagnostic read. This was a general overview of the plot. It was extremely helpful and reasonably priced. I then, for a fee, had him edit the first fifty pages. Again, this was very educational and I was able to get a good sense of how to proceed with the remainder of the manuscript. Still, after I published the book, there were a ton of typos. I then had to reevaluate my strategy: Should I continue to edit myself or look for an editor? I re-edited and guess what? I'm getting the hang of it. Ultimately, finding an editor is your call. Dave King Editorial Services

Publishing Tip: With the proliferation of e-books, copyright infringement is increasing. Recently many authors have noticed their work on sites without their authorization. Below find a Copyright Infringement Notification I sent to Amazon. Shortly after it was received, Amazon took down the rogue Kindle. My name is Linda A. Lavid and I am the author who maintains all rights to my book (Name) (ISBN or Identifying number). The book is published by Full Court Press, an imprint of FCPressLLC which is my company. I have not authorized this book to be issued in a Kindle edition (ASIN). I have never uploaded this book, set a sale price, agreed to any trade discount, or made arrangements to make this a Kindle download. For the above reasons, it appears by my copyright has been infringed. Furthermore, I am the owner of an exclusive right that is allegedly infringed. I have a good faith belief that the use of the material in the manner complained of is not authorized by the copyright owner, its agent, or the law; and this notification is accurate. I acknowledge that under Section 512(f) any person who knowingly materially misrepresents that material or activity is infringing may be subject to liability for damages. Contact Information: Name Address City/State/Zip Tel. E-mail.

Website Tip: The ease of navigating a site is important. Static navigation bars along the side or top should be marked clearly. Keep the fonts, buttons uncomplicated and use short descriptive headings to where each link will take a visitor. Like hyperlinks, choose words that are content rich rather than *Page 2* or *Page 3*. Navigation links to other pages on your site can also be placed as hyperlinks in content areas. Another mode of navigation is by linking words/phrases to anchored areas on the same page. (Often seen with FAQs where topic links are listed, then when clicked, lead a visitor to more information.) If you do this, make it easy for a visitor to return to where the original link was placed. Regarding anchors, should your website design program not have this feature, you can use HTML to embed anchors into pages. HTML

Marketing Tip: After all your work – the writing, editing, publishing, marketing – you may think it's time to settle back with a Mai Tai. Unfortunately, no. The pipeline hungers for another terrific book.

*****

Index

Thanks for the interest in *Weekly Strategies for Writers*. I hope you have found the information helpful.

As a companion book consider:

Composition: A Fiction Writer's Guide for the 21 Century. Divided into two parts, the first part is on writing fiction. This section may be of help if you want to write fiction or are stalled along the way. The second part is on publishing your work with a subsidy publisher using Print-on-Demand technology.

Other books:

On Creative Writing. A stand alone e-book that is the first part of Composition. All profits go to the Niger Water Well Project.

Teddy Bear: A Short Story. A light humor/erotic story that is available for free.

Of the Dance/De la Danza is a dual language book (English/Spanish) of my short stories. Adult content.

Paloma: A Laurent & Dove Mystery. Someone is after a woman with three identities. But which identity is he/she after?

Rented Rooms: A Collection of Short Fiction. My first collection of published short stories. Author notes discuss my thoughts about each story.

Thirst: A Collection of Short Fiction. Characters, some quirky, others creepy, share their lives of passion. Author notes included.

101 Ways to Meditate: Discover Your True Self. Primer for those who want to learn how to meditate or expand their meditative practice.

The Simple Mechanic of Infinite Execution: A Short Story. Meta-fiction soon to be out as a novella.

For more information, visit my website.

If you have any questions/comments, feel free to email me...lindalavid@gmail.com

Starry Nights! Linda.

Made in the USA
Las Vegas, NV
18 September 2021